"What is most commonly seen as Religion is manmade (The Outer Shell). Spirituality is natural and is a part of us from birth (The Inner Essence). This book and class helps anyone of any belief, even those without a specific belief, find the core of who they are by exploring the core of Spirituality. It takes us away from the chaos of everyday life and puts us into Nature — our 'Natural' state of being." ❖ **Melissa Lea Beasley** *(Assistant Spirituality Professor)*

"Dr. Hilliard's discussion of spirituality is simultaneously thought-provoking and inspiring. He leads you on a journey to the self deep within to discover and develop the peaceful, purposeful life that we were all created to have." ❖ **Sandra Croff** *(Student)*

"Spirituality is not necessarily a term involving religion. Your spirit is your innermost being, the part which allows you to find meaning in everything you do. Dr. Hilliard teaches us to recognize this inner spirit and how to connect with it, allowing us to enjoy the journey rather than longing for the end." ❖ **Elizabeth Bonesio** *(Student)*

"Dr. Hilliard's spirituality course was unlike any other class I've taken. I've grown and learned more about myself through all the wonderful rituals and experiences. And reading this book helped me find myself as a person." ❖ **Bobbi Hemmen** *(Student)*

"It was awesome to escape life for a week to be surrounded by nature. We all were able to open up to each other and learn something from everyone there. It was the best class ever!" ❖ **Emily Cross** *(Student)*

"Dr. Hilliard's teachings will change your outlook on life and your relationship with the universe. It will help you see through the negativities of this world and find the positive aspects that are within you and everything surrounding your existence." ❖ **Danielle Patton** *(Student)*

"Because of the spirituality class I find myself more grateful for life's simple pleasures...like a good dance!" ❖ **James Darnell** *(Student)*

SPIRIT-RITUAL

Exploring Spirituality
Beyond the Sacred Veil

Dr. K. Mark Hilliard

HILLIARD
PRESS

SPIRIT-RITUAL
Copyright © 2006 by Dr. K. Mark Hilliard
ISBN 0-9717444-5-9

Edited by Jessa Rose Sexton
Cover photos and concept by Melissa Lea Beasley
Author Photo by David Abbott of the Motion Picture Alliance, Inc.
Book Design by Paula Rozelle Bagnall

Published by:
Hilliard Press
A Division of the Hilliard Institute for Educational Wellness
Franklin, Tennessee
Oxford, England
www.hilliardinstitute.com

Also by Dr. K. Mark Hilliard:
THE CATCHER OF DREAMS:
A Holistic Approach to Wellness Therapy

Coming soon:
EDUCATIONAL WELLNESS:
A Holistic Approach to the Art & Science of Teaching & Learning

This book is dedicated to....

2004 Spirituality Class
Back L to R: Rachel McConnell, Dr. K. Mark Hilliard *(Professor)*, Bobbi Hemmen, Kathy Sandler, Audra Morris, Sandra Croff. **Front L to R:** Danielle Patton, Melissa Lea Beasley *(Assistant Professor)*, James Darnell.

2005 Spirituality Class
Back L to R: James Darnell, Marielle Jung, Jenny R. Peyton, Danielle Patton, Jack, Liz Bonesio, Heather Kennedy, Emily Cross. **Front L to R:** Jessica Allen, Sandra Croff, Dr. K. Mark Hilliard *(Professor)*, Melissa Lea Beasley *(Assistant Professor)*.

CONTENTS

PREFACE   iii

INTRODUCTION   v

DEFINITIONS   vii

STAGE ONE   1
   The Search

STAGE TWO   5
   Spirit, Soul, Mind, & Body

STAGE THREE   9
   The Sacred Veil

THE JOURNEY BEGINS   13
   One Assertion at a Time

ASSERTION ONE   15
   Opposites   17
   Antithetical Harmonization:
   Bringing Harmony to Opposites   22

ASSERTION TWO   33

    Conflict in Man   37

    Outline of the Areas of Physio-Spiritual Conflict   39

    Soul Wounds   40

    Signs of Soul Wounds   43

    Outline Comparing Physical Healing
    and Spiritual Healing   47

ASSERTION THREE   51

    Ritual   52

    Spirit-Ritual   54

    The Spirit-Ritual of Sex   57

    The Spirit-Ritual of the Spirit-Candle   59

    The Spirit-Ritual or Prayer   60

    The Spirit-Ritual for Removing the Presence of Evil   70

    The Spirit-Ritual of Worship   75

    The Spirit-Ritual for Creating a Sacred Place   77

    The Spirit-Ritual for Healing   79

    Spirit-Rituals for the Senses   82

    The Spirit-Ritual of Marriage   95

    The Spirit-Ritual of Romance   98

    The Name Giving Spirit-Ritual   99

    The Spirit-Ritual of Exercise   100

    The Give-Away Spirit-Ritual   102

    The Spirit-Ritual of Detachment   103

    The Spirit-Ritual of Going to Water   110

    The Spirit-Ritual of Meditation: 113

    Spirit-Rituals in Nature and the Creation: 118

    The Spirit-Ritual of Communion—the Circle   123

    Spirit-Rituals for Daily Activities   130

The Heyoka Spirit-Ritual   130
The Spirit-Ritual of Offerings   131

ASSERTION FOUR   135
Sacred Service — A Call to Higher Motives   137
Sacred Kindness — Finding Beauty in All
Living Things   140
Pure Love For All Things Created   142
Authentic Bliss   146

ASSERTION FIVE   151
Eightfold Pathway to Enlightenment   153

STAGE FIVE   156
The Journey Expressed
Spirituality — A Way of Life, Not a Movement   159
My Journey   163

STAGE SIX   169
Major Spiritual Movements   169
Hinduism   170
Buddhism   177
Confucianism and Taoism   175
Philosophical Belief   178
Native American Beliefs   179
Judaism, Islam, and Christianity   181

BIBLIOGRAPHY   191

❖ ❖ ❖

"Our age is retrospective. It builds the sepulchers of the fathers. It writes biographies, histories, and criticism. The foregoing generations beheld God and nature face to face; we, through their eyes. Why should not we also enjoy an original relation to the universe? Why should not we have a poetry and philosophy of insight and not of tradition; and a religion by revelation to us and not the history of theirs?"

Ralph Waldo Emerson (1836)

❖ ❖ ❖

I think, not, that Emerson speaks of a total disregard of the traditions of our ancestors, but of an awareness that our Creator is alive and well, speaking to His creation today. For does not the sun still shine upon man and with its holy radiance does not enlightenment still enter man's soul? It, then, is up to man to absorb this light and reflect forth its brilliance to our present age.

K. Mark Hilliard (2005)

PREFACE

In the Creation of the world the spiritual and physical aspects of the creation originally lived in perfect harmony. At the fall of man, directed by the human desire to be God, the two realms (spiritual and physical) were separated, and man could no longer enter the spiritual realm, physically. A great veil was formed between the two planes of being. Ever since that point in time a man or woman experiencing the touch of God will spend an entire lifetime trying to journey home through this veil. The pathway is narrow, and few there are who will find it, but for those who do, it is the journey beyond days.

INTRODUCTION

Spirit-Ritual: Exploring Spirituality Beyond the Sacred Veil is intended to represent a spiritual journey of thought and inspiration. It is to be read as my philosophical treatise on what I have found to be a physically unfathomable field of study. Within these pages are documented expressions of authentic truth as well as the ponderings of an array of spiritual explorers, of which I am merely one. Explorers from the distant past and yesterday will share their findings through the channel of my thoughts. Introductions will be made into a variety of spiritual belief systems and the individuals who influenced them, particularly drawing on the areas of similarity. It is my hope that the reader will find a mixture of intellectual reasoning and spiritual wonderment, Biblical revelation and religious philosophy, time-honored tradition and innovation ritual.

A common mistake often made by spiritual seekers is in focusing in on a specific "spiritual movement" for answers, rather than patiently searching for universal, authentic truth. And universal truth must point the seeker beyond the movement or the movement leader. It must point back to the Source — the Creator of all that is spiritual.

To truly be an explorer, one must look without, within, above, and beyond. One must be challenged to move outside the comfort zone of current knowledge and understanding. To do otherwise, is to reject the journey that leads beyond the sacred veil. And it is truly sad when we settle for a myth, when the truth is within our grasp.

"We can recognize our prejudices and illusions only when, from a broader psychological knowledge of ourselves and others, we are prepared to doubt the absolute rightness of our assumptions and compare them carefully and conscientiously with the objective facts" (Jung, 1959, pp. 114-115).

DEFINITIONS

One unique aspect of philosophy and religion is that they often use ordinary words, but with extraordinary meaning. I likewise have a tendency to individually assign meaning to words I use. Therefore, I will supply a brief list of such terms and their meaning within my personal philosophy.

Actuality: What something is, now.

Aesthetic Super-Consciousness: Bringing into our awareness the beauty in art and nature—the creation.

Altruism: Serving others.

Apperception: Our awareness of the spiritual, a perception of mystery.

Authentic Truth: Truth which has as its source First Cause. This truth will stand the test of time, but will often become inter-mingled with non-truth, sometimes to the point where the two are indistinguishable. Authentic Truth should be supported by historically documented evidence, but still requires a certain amount of faith since the observer has not, typically, witnessed the truth at its conception.

Causative Effect: One thing brings about another.

Egoism: Serving self.

Epistemology: The study or theories of knowledge.

First Cause: Every cause, every motion has a pre-cause, a pre-motion. Something places it into being or into motion. There is, however, Original First Cause, which is the authentic source of all other causes—God.

Metaphysical: Beyond the physical.

Music of the Spheres: Non-earthly sounds.

Mystic: One who seeks knowledge through mystery.

Oneness with God: We do not become God. We do not become Deity in any form. Rather the goal is to achieve a state of harmony with God. To become "like" God in our thoughts and actions, as we are so directed.

Potentiality: What something can become.

Religion: In it original form it was fairly synonymous with spirituality. In its truest form it has now come to mean an internal belief system which drives us toward outward action. In its most common form it now represents institutionalized spirituality.

Ritual: Mental or physical activities which symbolically analogize individual spiritual significance through their ceremonial form and purpose.

Sacredicity: The extent to which something has been made sacred.

Six Senses/Sixth Sense: Most speak of the five physical senses: seeing, hearing, touching, tasting, and smelling. The sixth sense refers to the awareness of the spiritual, a perception of mystery—apperception. But actually it is the five senses being experienced on a higher plane, rather than an auxiliary sense.

Spirituality: The growth and development of the inward man (spirit and soul). This progression takes place through our sacred service to others and as we come in contact with that which is sacred through ritual.

Tranquility of Mind: A peace and calm beyond our physical ability to comprehend.

Transcend: To move beyond the physical plane.

Vibrations: Physical and spiritual energy waves created by words, thoughts, feelings, and actions.

STAGE ONE

The Search

Each of us has an inner yearning to explore. A metaphysically inherited eagerness to discover the world in which we live and the world beyond. A drive to examine the physical realm, for which science sometimes supplies the answers. And a secret longing to delve even deeper, into the metaphysical or spiritual realm, where science seldom travels, and when it does, often fails in its futile attempts to explicate.

I am convinced this yearning is our individual spirit calling out to our material mind. Asking it to seek and find—inviting the realm of physical knowledge and reason to travel to the depths of our spirit and soul in search of resolve. It is a call home. A call to know our creator, to understand our purpose, to seek out meaning for our lives. A call to find our vocation, our true happiness, our contentment, fulfillment, joy, and peace—our Bliss. Yet often as we look to modern versions of Judeo-Christian religions, we are "turned off" by the prevailing hype, or the "old time" legalism. Or as we are swept away by the excitement and attraction that commonly occurs with an exploration into the philosophies of eastern religions or Native American spirituality, we soon drift away, feeling lonely and detached. We lose the connection, if we ever had it, and feel out of place and unfulfilled. We are confused, disappointed, and spiritually, mentally, and physically worn out. We just cannot seem to find what it is for which we seek. So we quit the journey, we secure our hearts from the perception of unearthly rhythm and sound, and we close the auditory canal of our spirits to the call. And with time the call fades. But with the fading of the call also comes the fading of the spirit.

Why? Why the disappointment, confusion, and pain? Why the lack of fulfillment? Why does the journey end without the destination in sight? Because as we observe modern religion's answer to spirituality, both eastern and western adaptations, it seems to have become nothing more than a materialistic, for-profit, institutionalized phenomenology—an extraordinary message delivered in a industry-like format, akin to any other business—and that is not what our spirit seeks. In truth, that is not what pure spirituality and uncorrupted religion was ever designed to be. [When discussed as a whole, spiritual movements such as Buddhism, Hinduism, Taoism, and Confucianism will be noted as eastern religions; when discussed as a whole, movements such as Judaism, Christianity, Islam (Moslem), or Native American spirituality will be referred to as western religions, even though much of their history can be traced back to a middle-eastern origin].

In the words of James, the brother of Jesus, around the year A.D. 48: "Pure and undefiled religion in the sight of our God and Father is this: to visit orphans and widows in their distress and to keep oneself unstained by the world" (NASB, 1995, James 1:27).

True spirituality and pure religion is not going to church three times a week in a multimillion dollar cathedral. It is not becoming a monk and leaving the world to enter a monastery. It is not a hierarchy of clergy and laity. It is not ritual for ritual's sake —be it Buddhism, Hinduism, Taoism, Confucianism, Judaism, Christianity, Islam, Native American spirituality or philosophy. And it is not a list of dos and don'ts to punish us for wrong doing and praise us for doing good.

❖ ❖ ❖

Pure, unadulterated religion is an internal sacred system of belief which guides us to serve others and to grow beyond the physical. It is spirit and soul seeking, and mind and body substantiation. It is a process through which the spirit, soul, mind, and body can be guided in becoming ONE in thought and deed and ONE with the Creator from whom they were formed.

❖ ❖ ❖

Religion is the roadmap to spirituality. It is an external expression of our inward beliefs. Any religion that does not point toward spiritual growth through God, service, unity, and keeping oneself unstained by the world, is not authentic. For our conviction is not to be "a" religion, or "any" religion, but "pure" religion, which guides us homeward.

Our Creator has placed within each one of us a spirit and a soul who recognize their Creator. A spirit and soul who, if we will allow them, if we learn to listen to them, will lead us on a journey that is out of this world. A journey beyond the sacred veil, where the astonishing clear vision of spirituality is to be found. But, to take this journey, we must first create a personal relationship with these entities. Our physical must connect with our own spiritual — our mind with our spirit, our body with our soul. We must become skilled in the art of oneness, and in so doing, we find the domicile of contentment and joy; we encounter the dwelling place of bliss. To reject this call is to exist in a world of suffering, without hope of joyful participation, to inhabit a land where man's soul will forever be lost in the hours of darkness.

STAGE TWO

Spirit, Soul, Mind, & Body

Our spirit is often associated with our inward emotions, feelings, and qualities (EFQ's), and rightly so. The spirit, however, is not synonymous with these EFQ's, but rather it is the place from whence our EFQ's are formed—the nativity of our true identity.

❖ ❖ ❖

Our spirit is our spiritual mind—the thinking, feeling, responding element of our inward being. Our spirit is the mind of our soul.

❖ ❖ ❖

Just as we have a physical mind housed within our body, we have a spiritual mind housed within our soul. And the heart is the center of this spirit. Within the physical mind resides a conscience that tells us right from wrong and directs us to do certain things, certain ways. But this physical mind and physical conscience are materialistically directed by reciprocal desires and selfish fears. We act in order to gain something in return or to avoid negative consequences. With the spirit and heart, we act for the pure pleasure of bringing joy to another person. We act because it is simply the right thing to do. At the soul level, we *know* the appropriate response.

❖ ❖ ❖

The Spirit is to the Soul, what the Mind is to the Body.

❖ ❖ ❖

Our soul is our spiritual body. It is the real person, the inward being—our metaphysical stability. The soul is our spiritual structure, our meta-matter, the foundation of our true essence. Our physical body is only a covering, swathed atop the true essence. It is simply an outward representation of the inward person, yet the means by which the soul actively maneuvers throughout this physical world. Beyond the veil lies the spiritual authenticity of our mind and body—the home place of our spirit and soul.

Yet, while life within our body lies, each of these spirit-identities remains encased within the confines of the human frame. Each locked away without a consistent existence in the homeland of the soul, nevertheless seeking constant release. What means exists for an escape?

Just as mentality and physicality involve the growth and development experiences of the mind and body, spirituality involves the growth and development experiences of the spirit and soul. Spirituality requires the creation of oneness in the relationship of spirit and soul, with mind and body; oneness with our Creator; oneness with the creation—including other people and the world of nature; oneness with worldly things—the things the world deems important; and oneness with our calling, our vocation, our purpose (Hilliard, 2002).

Spirituality also entails deliberate contact with that which is sacred. And sacredicity is justified by two standards: (1) that which has life force (spirit) within and/or (2) that which is of God, from God, or set apart for God. That which is of God includes our inward characteristics, the fruits of our spirit. That which is from God consists of life and the blessings that flow from life. And that which is set apart for God can be anything we choose (marriage, a period of time, money).

Mankind is thereby composed of a material organization solidified by a metaphysical structuring. Left to the design of the mind and body alone, we will remain in a state of division and imperfection. But, under the guidance of the spirit and soul, mankind can be lifted to a higher plane of existence wherein the astonishing manifestation of unity may be revealed. For the highly individualized spirit of man, while radically particular, is essentially similar, and if we will but listen, we will all hear the call. And the call will reveal the personal journey we each must take to explore beyond the veil. And, just perhaps, the self-imposed restraints which bind our spirit and soul will be loosed. "The spirit conceives neither seasons nor distances nor any other limiting definitions" (Hill, R.B., 1959, p. 105). [In her epic book, *Hanta Yo*, Ruth Beebe Hill took historic information collected from stories depicted on animal skins discovered in 1865. The story of an actual Mahto Indian family was created, translated into Lakota, then back into English under the title, *Hanta Yo — Clear the Path*].

STAGE THREE

The Sacred Veil

At the Heart of my Spiritual Philosophy are Five Assertions:

Assertion One—There are two realities, two aspects of life, two opposing realms divided by a sacred veil, yet coexisting side by side. Both sides are real and affect our daily lives. Whether or not we believe in them, and whether or not we understand them, is irrelevant to the reality of their existence. However, our belief and understanding are astronomically important to our ability to find meaning and purpose in life. This side of the veil is the physical realm—that which can be seen, understood, and proven by science, our five physical senses, and visual observation. The other side of the veil is the spiritual realm—that which many never see and understand and into which most others only obtain a small glimpse—the realm beyond the five senses, but into which the five senses may point the way.

These two realms are not separated by great vertical distances as some suppose—the physical realm way down here and the spiritual realm and heavens, way up above. Rather, the spiritual and physical are opposites existing here together as the inside and outside of the sacred veil, or the lower and higher planes of existence. The spiritual realm is difficult, if not impossible, to prove through typical scientific methodologies because it is not composed of visible, physical matter. But it is into this spiritual realm we must travel in order to find spiritual awakening, enlightenment, and bliss. Only in this higher plane will the answers to our true calling be found.

Assertion Two—All that has been created has spirit, or spiritual essence, and is eternally linked to both the physical and spiritual realms. All that has been created has physical life, and all that has physical life has a spirit or a spiritual essence which becomes clouded, cloaked, or veiled to our simple, physical observation and understanding. We only gain, or regain, insight into the other side of the veil as we begin to give up some of our physical notions of how things work and relinquish our unfounded beliefs in what is important in life. We must begin to search deep within ourselves as we also reach further outside of ourselves—outside of our circle of comfort and understanding. In many ways, we are to become as little children—full of wonder and awe, question and belief—yet coupled with the adult ability to utilize this newfound wisdom in securing our individual place in the universe.

Assertion Three—We are each born with the key, planted deep within our spirit, to open the doorway which leads beyond the veil. Through the pathway of spiritual ritual, we find this key. We not only have the ability to seek and connect, we have an obligation to our spirit, our soul, our mind, and our body. We are called by our spirit to take this journey. Our mind and body will battle, the world will wage war, religion will confuse, yet the voyage we must take. For to banish the call, to dismiss the journey, only allows us to *survive* our allotted days, not *live* them.

Assertion Four—Finding this key and beginning this journey is the only pathway to enlightenment. And bestowed upon the enlightened is the gift of true fulfillment—authentic bliss. As we begin our travels, we awaken our body and mind so that true enlightenment may take place, allowing us to reach the highest goal of our human existence—seeing the sacred beauty in, and experiencing pure love for, all things created. We are drawn by higher motives to take the gifts and talents with which we are blessed, grow and expand those gifts and talents, adjoin to them new gifts and talents, and share them with others in sacred service. By learning to share our true self, our spirit and soul, through the physical channel of an enlightened mind and body, we experience spiritual bliss.

Assertion Five—Just as we can be led to true enlightenment, true spirituality, we can also be led astray. Because of our desperation, we often fall prey to pseudo-spirituality. We get a glimpse of the spiritual realm, the sacred, but we (or others) physically pervert the vision to better meet our preconceived ideas, or our perceived needs and desires. We attempt to make the spiritual realm fit our physical ideology. What is sad is that through our manipulation of the sacred, we actually evade that which we truly seek. As we learn to look within—honestly search our depths, the center of our spirit (our heart)—we will find our true self, and that true self is eternally linked with the spiritual realm, from where our answers will befall. We must learn to listen with our heart as well as our ears, with our intuition as well as our powers of reason, with our spirit as well as our mind. We must learn to become One with both realms in order to transcend the veil.

❖ ❖ ❖

THE JOURNEY BEGINS

One Assertion at a Time

❖ ❖ ❖

ASSERTION ONE

There are two realities, two aspects of life,
two opposing realms divided by a sacred veil,
yet coexisting side by side.

"Always make it a practice to stir your own mind
thoroughly to think through what you have easily
believed. Your position is not really yours until
you make it yours through suffering and study. The
teacher from whom you learn the most is not the
one who teaches you something you didn't know
before, but the one who helps you take a truth with
which you have quietly struggled, give it expression,
and speak it clearly and boldly" (Chambers, 1992,
December 15).

❖ ❖ ❖

[Oswald Chambers was born in 1874 in Scotland. He studied at London's
Royal College of Art, the University of Edinburgh, and Dunoon College.
His life's calling was a spiritual teaching ministry in Japan, the United
Kingdom, and the United States].

A truly holistic view of the world recognizes the antithetical reality
of life. Everything has its opposite — its counterpart. This does not imply

that every opposing side is either negative or positive (although this is frequently the case), but that opposites are sometimes simply reverse sides of the same object, or inside versus outside. The Chinese philosophy of yin/yang is a perfect example of this precept, which holds that opposites are actually necessary for there to be order in the universe.

Whatever the type of opposite, a spiritual journey begins by examining diverging aspects of our individual lives and striving to recreate the balance and harmony required for oneness. Buddhist tradition speaks of the "Middle Path" or the mid-point between opposites. Other than the concept of necessary opposites, my philosophy differs somewhat from this tradition in that I believe we must often move entirely to the other side of the opposite in order to experience the sacred. I do, however, believe we must seek to understand both sides, even if one is negative, in order to maintain physio/spiritual equilibrium.

By looking at opposites in our everyday lives, we begin to better comprehend the coexisting aspect of divergences, which first allows us to believe in the sacred veil, then to see beyond. All around us are physical representations of the spiritual, yet to our witness they remain in shroud, because we inspect with the eyes of our mind, not the eyes of our spirit. We must also come to understand that what we do to one extremity in this antithetical chain will directly affect the opposite end. This spiritual principle is supported by the scientific findings of Isaac Newton's Third Law of Motion: for every action there is an equal and opposite reaction.

Opposites

Left	Right
Physical	Spiritual
Secular	Sacred
Time	Eternity
Earth	Heaven
Man	God
Mind	Spirit
Body	Soul
Conscience	Heart
Man-made	Natural
Worldly	Holy
Night	Day
Darkness	Light
Unknowing	Enlightened
The Seen	The Unseen
Conscious	Unconscious
Asleep	Awake
Empty	Full
Solid	Liquid
Distort	Clarify
Death	Life
Sickness	Health
Weakness	Strength
Devastate	Heal
Crave	Resist
Addiction	Control
Evil	Good

Wrong	Right
Doubt	Believe
No	Yes
False	True
Deny	Accept
Take	Give
Partial	Whole
Tear Down	Build
Destroy	Create
Hold	Release
Attach	Detach
Retain	Renounce
Negative	Positive
Sad	Happy
Revenge	Forgiveness
Jealousy	Trust
Hate	Love
Turmoil	Peace
Discord	Unity
Depress	Raise Up
Mean	Kind
Unfaithful	Faithful
Discord	Harmony
Separate	Together
Distant	Close
Complex	Simple
Sitter	Doer
Fast	Slow
Impatient	Patient
Worry	Trust

Harsh	Gentle
Greedy	Generous
Selfish	Selfless
Curse	Bless
Talk	Listen
Send	Go
Ignore	Study
Justice	Mercy
Destination	Journey
Have	Do
Observe	Participate
Give Up	Endure
To Be Served	To Serve

❖ ❖ ❖

"Every act of our life strikes some chord that will vibrate into eternity" (Warren, 2002, p. 7).

❖ ❖ ❖

[Rick Warren wrote the now popular book, *The Purpose-Driven Life*, a book designed to help individuals find Godly derived purpose and meaning in life].

Everything we physically do and say creates vibrations. These vibrations go out into the universe and affect those around us today and forever—from now into eternity. And any vibrations that go out, must first start their rhythm within: we are first and foremost affected by our thoughts and actions. The vibrations of good collect within and go forth to accomplish good without, opening doors to the sacred. The vibrations of evil collect and go forth to destroy, opening doors to the anti-sacred. Have you ever been in a place where "love was in the air," or felt the uneasiness of being "in the presence of evil?" These are more than simple catch phrases. They are a vibrational reality.

With this vibratory process in mind let us now consider the spirit of man. Could it be that the same method of transport is utilized by the spirit? Throughout the history of spiritual writings, the words "in spirit" have been repetitively used to denote accomplishing something, or being with someone else, in-spirit. Just as the mind and body create vibrations, would not it seem likely that the spirit and soul also create vibrations? As we learn to connect with and comprehend our spirit, its thoughts, words, and actions create these vibrations, which go out from us as "spirit in action." Our spirit, while residing within our body, also travels outward on spiritual vibrations, allowing us to "pray in-spirit," "be with someone in-spirit," or "leave a bit of our spirit" behind in something we create—be it a piece of furniture, a painting, a letter, music, or a poem. Then as someone encounters our spirit vibrations, they are touched—they feel *a* presence. And if they have the spiritual capability to decode the vibratory motion, they are moved—they feel *our* presence.

At whatever level our vibrations are expressed, we and those around us create our own personal environment for physical and spiritual growth, or physical and spiritual decay, by the chords we strike. And we construct our ability to believe and understand this process through our willingness to explore opposites. In simple terms, as we conduct ourselves in positive ways which are the opposite of our normal actions, we will be able to, quite obviously, note how our personal changes affirmatively affect the responses of those with whom we come in contact—we will begin to comprehend our constructive vibratory effect on others.

To set in motion this ability to gain glimpses into the spiritual realm, we must first learn to fine-tune our mind and body so that they are in harmony with our spirit and soul. In principle, to understand the spiritual realm, we must create physical analogies which represent spiritual ideology.

Whereas an active spirit and soul can activate the mind and body to respond, an active mind and body can likewise activate the spirit and soul. "Good for the body is the work of the body, good for the soul the work of the soul, and good for either the work of the other" (Thoreau, 2000, p.32). [Henry David Thoreau (1817-1862) and Ralph Waldo Emerson were two of New England's greatest transcendentalist philosophers. Thoreau is probably best known for *Walden* and his *Essay on Civil Disobedience*].

❖ ❖ ❖

The interconnected relationship between these entities (spirit, soul, mind, body) allows each the opportunity to awaken the other. By intently examining physical experiences, we form a union of understanding between spirit and mind. By taking part in these experiences, we create union of soul and body.

❖ ❖ ❖

Though the process is simple, the difficulty in proceeding is often great. In most cases, we must move from the left toward the right in our field of opposites. We have to move away from that which draws our mind and body, toward that which draws our spirit and soul. And since, in the beginning, we might not understand or even believe in the spirit and soul, we must move toward that which addresses moral excellence—the greater good—even in the face of fear or desire. Likewise, we might not wish to move toward the greater good, a call of the physical mind, not the spirit. These obstacles then present themselves as our first opposites to overcome—a lack of understanding, disbelief, and self-centeredness. "The seat of faith is not consciousness but spontaneous religious experience, which brings the individual's faith into immediate relation with God" (Jung, 1959, p. 100). [Dr. C. G. Jung, born in Switzerland in 1865, was one of the pioneers of modern day psychiatry, along with Freud and Adler].

So this is where one makes the decision to accompany me on this spiritual journey or to put this book down and retreat back into the world of the physical—never experiencing that which is on the other side of the veil. To continue with success requires a commitment to change, and change is not that easy for most of us because we are so set in our ways. And as for commitment, few have any idea what it means. We are a generation of quitters. If we don't like something, we simply quit—be it a job, a marriage, or a responsibility.

The reality is, our lifestyles don't require commitment to survive—which is all most of us do. But to live, to truly be who we are intended to be, to find meaning, purpose, and joy in life, we must be willing to change and commit.

Antithetical Harmonization:
Bringing Harmony to Opposites

Up to this point I have used the pronouns "we" and "our." For the purpose of personalizing this activity, I will hereafter—within this section—use the pronoun "you."

In order to create wellness (well-being of the whole person—spirit, soul, mind, and body), you must begin to recognize the opposite or other side of your personal reality. In fact, wellness requires the balance or harmony of opposites. To begin the process, you should create a personal list of opposites by examining beliefs, emotions, fears, personality traits, habits, talents, likes, dislikes, etc. (similar to the list on pages 17–19). Once the list is created, it may be supplemented at any time.

The simple format for this exercise is to examine where you are and then examine the opposite. If the greater good is at the opposite extremity, you must create opportunities, exercises, and rituals which will move you in that direction. And remember, the greater good is not what you desire, rather what will bring about positive internal vibrations which can then go out into the universe and strike positive cords of peace, joy, and fulfillment in others. As you accept and transmit these positive vibrations, you simultaneously reject the influence of negative vibrations.

If it is a belief system you are examining, then you must test the spirits to assure their truth. You scrutinize your convictions against other belief systems for authenticity, and you listen for the response of your heart to the message. You are not seeking a movement to follow, but a universal truth to accept.

And yes, even when your mind and body do not wish to participate, you go forth, accepting the verity that through your action will come understanding, through your understanding will come belief, and through your belief will come vision beyond the sacred veil—a spirit-guided exploration into the spiritual realm.

Let it be known that for everything that draws you away, there is something to draw you back. For every illness, there is a healing agent. For everything good, there is an equivalent evil. For everything you see, there is that which you do not see. This tenet should help you appreciate the necessity to make sure you are where you need to be, rather than simply where you have been placed.

Exercises in Opposites:
If you have a difficult time believing in the spiritual, it is usually a sign that you spend most of your time dealing with the physical. You must commit one hour (more or less) each day to examining that which is spiritual, and you must do so with an open mind—go to this study without any preconceived ideas of what you will find. Read spiritual material like it was the first time you were ever exposed to it and pray for understanding. Read if for yourself, without commentaries or reviews from others. Let it speak to you personally. Authentic truth is alive. When examined without predetermined, rigid boundaries, it should stir you at the core of your

spirit. If you are not moved, the spiritual material you are reading is either not authentic, or you have yet to open your mind to your spirit.

If you are one who is self-centered or selfish, you must take the focus off of yourself—find someone who has a need and fulfill it without their knowledge. Spend some time everyday providing acts of random kindness. Random act of kindness include making a visit, sending a card, mowing a yard, or giving a gift, etc.

 If you have lack of confidence as you attempt to get something you need from a boss, a friend, or an employee, repeat in your mind a mantra of trust, belief, and other positive thoughts. If on your mind are thoughts of anger, distrust, or lack of confidence, you will send out vibrations of such and in return receive the same. If you create a vibrational atmosphere of positive energy, you can likewise expect to receive positive responses. Does this mean that you will always get what you desire? No, but you will, more often, get what you need.

If you are drawn toward what you know to be wrong, you must place into your life specific opportunities to do right and avoid those circumstances that direct you toward wrong: if there is an individual with whom you have a difficult time doing right, you must avoid such union. If there is someone with whom you are close, make an accountability pact: when you are tempted to do wrong you must first contact him or her and share what you are considering doing.

If you desire revenge, you must create avenues to offer forgiveness— even if you do not desire to do so and even if the object of your revenge makes no such requests. You can send a card, offer a prayer, or share a blessing. And always examine your own need for forgiveness, for there is someone to whom all of us are indebted. It is difficult to remain revengeful toward someone you are constantly praying for and likewise difficult upon examining your own state of impoverished purity.

If you feel the pain of hate, you must find someone to love and someone toward whom you can outwardly show love—you must utilize visual representations of love. You must also seek to find someone who loves you for who you are and who shows you love through visual forms—an important component of a belief in a personal God. Only love can destroy hate. And as with all opposites which are emotional in nature, you must understand that you first experience the emotions before you share them—if you share love, you first feel the power and strength of that love; if you share hate, the initial pains of that hate create personal distress within you long before they are ever shared, and long thereafter.

If you have been unfaithful, you must set up opportunities to be faithful, rather than opportunities to be unfaithful. Arrange specified and regular quality time with the one with whom you should be faithful—and make it happen. Romance is not meant to depart upon marriage; rather, it is meant to evolve into something even more meaningful, for it is now based on commitment.

If you find yourself impatient, you must practice patience. Find ways to delay gratification in areas where it is not really important, in order to prepare your mind and body for delayed gratification in more serious matters.

If you talk too much, set aside a period of time and only listen—be it one hour or one day—with no speech whatsoever.

If you live a fast-paced lifestyle, then find a few simple activities that require you to slow down—perking your coffee rather than using a coffee maker, slow cooking a meal rather than using the microwave, taking a long bath rather than a shower, driving the scenic route rather than using the interstate. Make a ritual out of the now unhurried activity by finding meaning in the format.

If you lie, make a pact to only tell the truth for one day—the whole truth, no white lies or half truths. This does not, however, give you the right to be insensitive to the feelings of others; these situations call for times of silence. If you find yourself tempted to lie, journal about the situation, your feelings, and why you wished to lie. And think before you allow yourself to be backed into a corner—a position in which man will inevitability respond negatively, out of self-defense.

If you are depressed, you must lift yourself up, by lifting someone else up. When depressed, you must find someone who needs your help and help them—the most absolute opposite of you being down, is someone else being lifted up. After first doing something to lift someone else up, you can then add things which lift you up. Laughter fits into the realm of opposites for depression, as well as listening to upbeat music. So go see a comedy, visit a humorous friend, rent a funny movie, or listen to bright and breezy melodies as you dance around the house. If you are surrounded by man-made buildings and machinery, spend a weekend in the woods—limit the man-made items you take with you to food, clothing, shelter, and possibly a good book.

If you drive everywhere you go, walk everywhere for one day. Or avoid travel altogether and spend the day at home.

If your life is all about a destination (career, retirement, new house, next year's vacation), you must change your perception by finding joy in your current circumstances or in the journey toward the destination. If you cannot find joy in the simple things, you will only find temporal joy in the big things. Examine pieces of your day and find those things which are pleasant—relish them, whether they be the morning coffee or saying prayers with your children before bed. Find meaning in the journey, or the destination will leave you feeling empty. A good exercise is to plan a trip where the emphasis is on the points in between the starting place and the journey's end. Stop at family inns and off-the-path restaurants and sites.

If you have caused any devastation (angry words, the killing of a life-form, physical abuse, etc.), then offer a healing hand (plant a tree, volunteer at a hospital, provide a kind word, or compliment someone). Do no harm for a whole day—don't even take the life of an ant or say a word which may be perceived as negative.

If you get angry at someone, analyze the anger and direct it toward what the person has done, not toward the person. Make sure your discussions are "I feel angry when you…" rather than "you make me angry." When you direct anger toward people, they become defensive. When anger is directed toward the wrong, there is hope for healing. You must think upon things you appreciate about those who upset you, rather than what makes you angry.

If you hold on too tightly, choose something you love and give it away. This may be an actual item, an idea, your time, always getting your way, or a tightly held habit.

If your world has become complex, busy, or overly full, then you need to physically simplify—go through your clothes and give away those that just sit on the shelf, clean out the garage, toss clutter from under the bed or in the closet. By simplifying your physical environment, you simplify your mental anxieties. By simplifying your mental anxieties, you open your mind to spiritual communication.

If your spouse is unpleasant in action and does things that irritate you, or if you are shown no respect, then do things in turn that are the opposite. Do things that create a pleasant atmosphere. You encourage, and you show respect, through your words and actions. With time, a vibratory reciprocal response will develop.

If you have a craving or addiction (something you feel you must have), you must resist it, even if only for short periods of time. If a strong craving, resist it for one hour (many cravings lessen within the first 10-20 minutes). If a weaker craving, work to resist it for one day at a time. This process may be as simple as resisting that urge to scavenge the cabinets for a snack before bed, or as complex as resisting a habitual addictive action such as smoking after every meal.

If your life is full of worries, then set aside a time, be it one dedicated hour a day or one weekend per month, and do something that is free of cares. Go on a weekend trip to the mountains—tell only one significant person how you may be contacted and turn the cell phone off. Have no schedule—sleep until you get up, eat when you're hungry, and make love in the middle of the day.

If your world is in turmoil, spend a day in quietness—no television, no phone, no outside contact, no speech. Get up before everyone else and observe the sun as it climbs above the horizon.

If you wish to curse someone or say something bad about him or her to others, then offer a blessing for his or her well-being. Say only the good things you can offer, or say nothing at all.

If you believe you are a good teacher, become a student for a semester. This can take place at a community college, a church or community center, or with the aid of a good book. An effective teacher must regularly place him/herself in the role of a student.

If you are a meat eater, become a vegetarian two days a week. Changing your diet is not only good physically; it can have soulful spiritual implications as well.

If you must be in control, choose a safe situation in which you give your control to another—a best friend, a spouse, a parent, a teacher, or a carnival ride.

If you always follow logic, follow your heart in a given situation. Just do what you think is right—what you would like happen to you.

If you are one who has many things, examine the way you spend your time. Often, if you have great things (big house, fine clothes, expensive cars) you work yourself to the point that you have no time to just be and do. And along with the many collected things, you will frequently find a collection of stress and debt. Those that do the things they enjoy don't always have the extra things in life, but they have the time to do what brings them joy and allows them time to spend with those they love. Forget that 80's philosophy of "quality time" and give yourself, and those you love, more quantity.

This sampling of opposites presents the principle you must follow to create antithetical harmonization. Take your current state of affairs and find the opposite. Think upon both ends of the pendulum, and if the greater good is opposite your typical approach, make a change—even if just for a short, committed, period of time. Then do it again, and again, and again. If the greater good is within your current approach, then make a commitment to understand the other side. For in understanding your opposites, even if the opposites are negative, you become less critical, less judgmental, and much more tolerant. Either way, you begin to find balance of opposites, encounter an increasing degree of wellness, and begin to open the pathway to your spirit which will allow its voice to be heard above the aimless distractions of your mind. And it is with your spirit as your guide that you travel into the other realm. In-spirit, you journey beyond the sacred veil.

This process of opposites may not seem natural, for many believe we should just accept who and what we are in order to be true to ourselves. But think upon this: is it really "unnatural" or simply "unworldly" to not go with the flow? I believe there is a significant difference in the natural and the worldly. Nature is what our physical being calls us to do. Worldly is what the influences of the world call us to do—which, in reality, are often very unnatural. Things like the love of money, envy, greed, hate, war, sexual perversions, or taking more than we need are essentially distortions of nature. Indeed, looking to our opposites can actually provide a pathway back to nature—nature as it was intended to be.

In *Civil Disobedience*, Thoreau stated that "if a plant cannot live according to its nature, it dies; and so a man (Thoreau, 2000, p. 39). I would alter this statement only slightly, asserting that if a plant cannot *adapt*, it dies; and so a man. For nature is not our true destination. Our true destination is our super-nature. While nature is what our physical being calls us to *do*, our super-nature, our spiritual-nature, is what our spirit calls us to *be*.

The story was told by Bear Heart of a young mom and dad who upon bringing home their new baby daughter from the hospital were asked by their five year old son if he could be alone with the baby for a few minutes. The parents agree, but stand, cautiously, just outside the bedroom door. The young boy walks over to his new sister, takes her hand, and looks intently into her enormous eyes. In a quiet voice the boy inquires of his baby sister, "Would you remind me about God, I'm beginning to forget" (Bear Heart, 1998). [Bear Heart is a full-blooded Muskogee Creek Indian, a medicine man, and a healer who shares his unique combination of Christian and Native American tradition through his lectures, writings, and work with the Memorial Psychiatric Hospital in Albuquerque, New Mexico].

The story of our personal creation is imprinted deep within our heart as the Creator lovingly breathes spirit into each new form. But as we go through this life the story gets clouded until, eventually, it becomes lost. We must journey back to our soul and find our story.

Carl Jung raised a probing question surrounding this whole concept of opposites—especially as it relates to man's spiritual conception. "Is the world of man and nature, the opposite of God" (Jung, 1957, p. 34-35)? While I do not believe the world was created as an opposite, but in its initial state of purity as an expression of God's beauty, I do believe the world has been, and still is, drawn "away from" God—drawn into opposition day by day. Thus, creating the bi-conditional situation in which the world can now only be saved by its opposite — throwing off the contrary and returning to the essence of the Creator.

ASSERTION TWO

All that has been created has spirit, or spiritual essence, and is eternally linked to both the physical and spiritual realms.

Our spirit, soul, mind, and body must become one through the process of examining opposites. But this process is only the first step in the sequential stages of becoming one with our Creator.

❖ ❖ ❖

Aristotle believed that all living things have psyche or soul and that this soul is what makes something alive. The lower levels of life such as plants have only the capability for the provision of sustenance and procreation, lower animals have the additional attributes of sensation and freedom of movement from one place to another on their own, higher animals add the capability to develop limited memory, and humans add to all these traits the capacity to reason. Aristotle's treatise on the soul also commented on the idea that at the soul level, all of humankind is the same—it is matter (our physical body) that makes one soul different from the other. The soul is created as a result of the initial creation of the body (Flew, Anthony, 1979).

Plato, on the other hand, believed that the soul existed before it inhabited the body. And as the soul wakes up within a new body it is confused, without remembrance. Then as the body goes through life, the soul is awakened by experiences which call it home (Gaarder, 1996). [Plato was a disciple of Socrates, known as the greatest of all philosophers. Plato lived from 428-348 B.C.; Aristotle was a student of Plato and lived from 384-322 B.C.].

I don't believe Aristotle was far from the truth, although Plato's understanding of an awakened soul, hearing the call home, also holds veracity. For from the sacred words of the Master Creator, "Let there be," and from the dust of the ground, all life-forms were fashioned. In the Genesis story of creation the Creator took dust from the ground and created a physical body with a physical mind. He then breathed life [spirit] into that physical form, and it became a living soul (Genesis 2:7). A soul it became once spirit was breathed into it by the Creator—supporting the concept that the soul is a unique creation because of the action of the Creator breathing life/spirit into the human form. And I believe this still happens today.

As for the notion of a soul in a non-human life form, we have no straightforward reply, but we at least have support for a spirit or spiritual essence in all living matter—depending on the appropriate interpretation of the word translated as both "spirit" and "breath" in Psalms 104:29 and elsewhere, and based on the meaning of the word "life." In fact, I have found that all religions acknowledge, on some level, this aspect of spirit or spiritual essence found in created life forms, with Celtic and Native American traditions often referring to animals as soul friends or spirit helpers.

"O Lord, how many are Your Works! In wisdom You have made them all; The earth is full of your creatures…They all wait for You to give them their food in its appointed time. You give to them, they gather it up; You open Your hand, they are satisfied with good. You hide Your face, they are dismayed; You take away their spirit, they expire and return to their dust. You send forth Your Spirit they are created; and You renew the face of the ground" (NASB, 1995). [From the book of Psalms 104:24-30 — the ancient book of prayer and praise which at its core recognizes God, the Creator, as the Center of the Universe, 1100-930 B.C.].

And from another ancient Biblical text: "For everything created by God is good, and nothing is to be rejected if it is received with gratitude; for it is sanctified [made sacred] by means of the word of God and prayer" (NASB, 1995 — I Timothy 4:4-5). [Written in A.D. 64 to Timothy (a faithful follower of The Way of The Christ) from Paul, called to be an apostle and set apart (made sacred) for the purpose of sharing the Good News of how to reconnect with our Creator].

If accepted as authentic truth, these early writings ascertained that all things created have a sacred/spiritual essence, since all things, from the "word of God," were spoken into existence. Therefore, there must be a passageway through which a connection can be made between the physical being and the spiritual being.

As for the meaning of the word "life" (portrayed as "creatures" in Psalms 104) to which a spirit is supplied, most philosophers would render the term as including plant life and higher forms. Native Americans typically denote the term as encompassing all that is created, including soil, stone, air, and water, even though some of these elements are not considered to have the ability to move or nourish themselves (a point which might be argued). Some, though, believe that the spirit, or soul, are only entities of human life.

In order to gain insight into this sacred life essence called spirit and soul, in order to travel the pathway to sacred wisdom, we must look outside our circle of earthly knowledge and understanding, into the hallowed realm of the spiritual. "Get away from your rational system and get into the wonderful experience that is moving through all things all the time. It is through living that we experience and communicate the spirit" (Campbell, Joseph, as selected in Osbon, 1991, p.206). [Joseph Campbell is best known for his message of "following one's bliss." He was the world's foremost authority on mythology—a professor, writer, and modern day philosopher].

Surrounding each of us there is a circle of identity, and our perception of the world is formulated by our individual circle. This distinctive hoop is shaped by our cultural and life experiences; the countries, states, and cities in which we have lived; our parents; our schooling and personal education practices; and our daily environment. In most instances, our circle has hypnotized us into the way we think and what we believe. It is only when we push our life experiences beyond our circle that we communicate with our spirit and the spirit of all things created. Because no matter how big our physical circle becomes, it is self-limited by our corporeal boundaries—the outside of our circle will always be bigger. We must, therefore, constantly work to expand our physical boundary into the realm of the metaphysical.

A circle bound by physical limitations cannot reflect the light of understanding found in the spiritual realm—we cannot become enlightened while bound within our self-limiting circle. Even though some of our views and actions might be labeled as spiritual, they are seldom more than a reflection of the views of our sphere—its morals, beliefs, religion. But as our spirit is aroused, as our heart is pricked, we begin to question these views. And for many of us this arousal creates fear, or at least discomfort. This physical apprehension causes most people to shut down and simply maintain their spirituality on a mere physical level—existing within the limits of their self imposed circle. But blessed be the one who steps beyond. Exalted is he who finds the eternal link and pursues its path.

Our connection with the sacred brings with it both good and bad. As physical beings, we experience the joys and suffer the consequences of the way in which we live, now. These consequences will also affect us when our physical life is gone and only our spirit and soul remain. Everything we do to one part of our being while living in this world, affects the other—what we do with our body affects our soul, what we do with our mind affects our spirit, and vice versa. This means that unless we bring enlightenment to our physical being, we will suffer the consequences far into eternity. Unless we settle the physio-spiritual conflict within, and heal the world-imposed wounds of the spirit and soul, our link to the eternal will only bear us pain.

Conflict in Man

A warring conflict is created within the human body between the spiritual and the physical entities—between the ethereal and the earthly, the mystical and the practical. The reality is that they independently desire different things. One is lured by the eternal link, the other by the temporal. One first hears the call of the heavens, while one hears the call of the world. The one that triumphs is the one that engages in the strongest combat. And the purpose for combat is not death, but surrender—to bring about unity by shifting the physical underneath, in harmony with, and surrendered to, the spiritual.

While the "old man" must die—the old way of thinking—neither aspect can totally disappear while we are yet physically alive. So we are seeking to create harmony, by bringing one under the authority, discipline, and control of the other.

As discussed within *Assertion One*, this conflict in man is created by antithetical dis-harmonization—disharmony of opposites. The primary disharmony appears when we attempt to follow both the spiritual and physical at the same time, for we cannot. The Apostle Paul wrote of this conflict in his theological transcript to those following The Way of The

Christ in Rome around A.D. 57 (Romans 8: 14-25). Paul wanted to provide hope to all people throughout time. His message identified an internal battle as a sign of spiritual life and energy. It is when the battle finally ceases that we must fear the outcome.

His words still speak volumes to those of us today who are fighting a good fight. "We know that the law [law of Moses] is spiritual. But I [physical man] am not spiritual. Sin rules me like I am its slave. I don't understand the things I [physical man] do. I don't do the good things I [spiritual man] want to do. And I [physical man] do the bad things I hate to do. And if I [spiritual man] don't want to do the bad things I [physical man] do, then that means that I [spiritual man] agree that the law is good. But I [spiritual man] am not really the one doing these bad things. It is sin living in me [physical man] that does these things. Yes, I know that nothing good lives in me [physical man]—I mean nothing good lives in the part of me that is not spiritual. I [spiritual man] want to do the things that are good. But I [physical man] don't do those things. I [physical man] don't do the good things I [spiritual man] want to do. I [physical man] do the bad things that I [spiritual man] don't want to do. So if I [physical man] do things I [spiritual man] don't want to do, then it is not really me [spiritual man] doing those things. It is sin living in me [physical man] that does those bad things.

"So I have learned this rule: When I [spiritual man] want to do good, evil is there with me. In my mind, [spiritual mind] I am happy with God's law. But I see another law working in my body [physical body]. That law [physical desire] makes war against the law [spiritual desire] that my mind [spiritual mind] accepts. That other law [physical desire] working in my body is the law of sin, and that law makes me its prisoner. This is terrible! Who will save me from this body [physical body] that brings me death? God will save me! I thank him for his salvation through Jesus Christ our Lord!

"So in my mind [spiritual mind] I am a slave to God's law. But in my sinful self I [physical man] am a slave to the law of sin" (Holy Bible, Easy-to-Read Version, 2000—Romans 7:14-25).

Conclusion: we must bring the sinful self (the physical mind and body) under the authority of spiritual self (spirit and soul) and we must bring spiritual self under the control of the Spirit of our Creator. Self-control, in essence, becomes Spirit-control. "One must go beyond the pairs of opposites to find the real source" (Joseph Campbell as selected in Osbon, 1991, p. 200).

Outline of the Areas of Physio-Spiritual Conflict

Physical Realm	Spiritual Realm
Physical mind—brain, conscience, nervous system, surface EFQ's	Spiritual mind—spirit, inward mind, heart, deep EFQ's
Physical body—chemical, physical desires and needs	Spiritual body—soul, eternal desires and needs
Sin and selfish desires	Spiritual desires, greater good, higher motives
The written Law, rules, dos/don'ts—forced obedience.	The Law of the Spirit, written on the heart—pure desire to do good
The façade, outside of the veil	The real you, beyond the veil
The two "I's/Me's"—sinful self, sin living in me	The two "I's/Me's"—Spiritual self, God living in me
Evil	Good
Prison, chains	Freedom

The answer to this conflict of opposites:

"Who will save me from this body [physical body] that brings me death? God will save me!" (Holy Bible, Easy-to-Read Version, 2000—Romans 7:25). The only resolve to the conflict in man is to reconnect with the Source of our creation and to be re-made in His image.

Soul Wounds

When physio/spiritual conflict is not resolved in a peaceful manner, and under the guidance of the Ultimate Peacemaker, the effect is often one of a wounded spirit and soul—hereafter called soul wounds.

❖ ❖ ❖

"She starts to weep. She has lost her soul. This is depression. This is loss of energy and joy in life. Something has Slipped out" (Campbell, Joseph, as selected in Osbon, Diane K., 1991, p.223).

❖ ❖ ❖

A soul wound occurs when over time we are attacked at the core of our inner-being and fail to aptly defend. Something within us begins to slide away, until it is lost. Depression sets in, and will not go away. With our mind and body we search for resolve, and resolve we do not find. And the spirit sleeps.

Some choose to hide in the darkness and let the blows assail upon them. Others respond with acts of violence. Not against those who cause them harm, but often on those they claim to love—routinely themselves. And the spirit sleeps.

Though the assaults may begin from without, the wounds occur from within—battle scars. The age-old struggle between the spirit and its pergola—the spirit and its place of dwelling. And the spirit sleeps.

There was a time when the spirit was our valiant warrior. Blades they swung, battles were won, spoils taken. And the spirit sleeps.

For the spirit, we allowed to slumber, its counsel we did fail to follow. And the spirit retreated, leaving us to ourselves defend. And this we could not do. For our soul, without the spirit at its defense, did easily wound. And the spirit sleeps.

"Where is my God?" we scream. "Why does He not defend me?" we plead. And the spirit sleeps.

But at last we finally bow. Oh spirit awaken and once again bridge the planes beyond the veil. Lead me to my God who alone can heal my wounds. And at last, the spirit arises, and calls upon the One who gave it breath, and we are wounded no more. (Hilliard, 2006).

❖ ❖ ❖

"Our fight is not against people on earth. We are fighting against the rulers and authorities and the powers of this world's darkness. We are fighting against the spiritual powers of evil in the heavenly places. That is why we need to get God's full armor. Then on the day of evil you will be able to stand strong. And when you have finished the whole fight you will still be standing" (Holy Bible, Easy to Read Version, 2000, Ephesians 6:12-13). [A letter from the Apostle Paul to believers in The Way of The Christ at Ephesus and to various churches in Asia. Probably written around A.D. 60 while Paul was imprisoned in Rome].

This writer to the Ephesians continues by noting the framework of this sacred armor. He lays out the analogy of utilizing the armor in the same order in which it would have been ritualistically applied before battle: *tightening the Belt of Authentic Truth around your waist* — this action was preparatory to putting on the armor because without a girded belt a warrior cannot run, fight, or otherwise be prepared to take part in battle (likewise, we must start with a solid foundation of authentic truth or we will not be appropriately prepared for life's battles); *over your chest and heart put on Righteousness*—this may either be right-living or being renewed and made right by God (either way, our heart must be right with God in order to receive His protection); *secure your feet in a firm foothold with the Good News of Peace*—in the Christian faith this is the way of being made right with God (we create an inner peace, through an active belief in the Anointed One, Christ, who came as God in the flesh); *use the Shield of Faith to stop the burning arrows of the evil one*—we must understand that our only true protection from soul wounds is a belief in, and dependence on, our Creator; *a Helmet of Salvation*—the home-place or center for our mind needs to be covered by the gift of saving grace, or it will be led by the ways of the world and suffer eternal loss (we must be forgiven and feel forgiveness or the pains of guilt and shame will beat us down); *the Sword of the Spirit of God, the Teaching or Word of God*—either the Spirit of God is the sword or the Word of God is the sword (either way, we are to equip ourselves with the teachings, and in-dwelling Spirit, of the One Who Made Us); and finally, as we put on the full armor of God, *we are to Pray in the Spirit*—our spirit must connect with the Spirit of God (His Spirit will intercede for our spirit, asking for strength, guidance, and deliverance).

This full-body armor then becomes, not only our protection for future battles, but our answer for previous battle wounds of the soul. For with this armor one can travel back, as well as forward, and heal those old wounds which inhibit our spiritual growth.

"Only when we are free of the past can we be fully alive in the present" (Walsh, 1999, p. 132). [Dr. Roger Walsh is professor of psychiatry, philosophy, and anthropology at the University of California at Irvine. The material shared in his book, *Essential Spirituality*, is based on more that twenty years of research into world religions and spirituality].

The religion of India calls the effects of past wounds on our soul *Karma*—the psychological and spiritual residue of prior actions and experiences.

Signs of soul wounds:

Common signs of soul wounds consist of: unresolved anger, fear, rage, bitter talk, emotional outbursts, shame, withdrawal, depression, suicidal tendencies, resentment, feelings of worthlessness and low self-esteem, lack of commitment, inability to hold a job, alcoholism and other substance abuse, numerous health problems, and acts of physical violence—often within one's own family and own community.

One theory behind this phenomenon, very common to Native American populations but also known among other populations and individuals at large, is that a culture or individual with significant soul wounds will not rise against its oppressor for fear of reprisal. Instead, the culture or individual, in anger and resentment, will rise against those with whom it can more readily inflict pain and suffering without immediate consequences—often close family members or self. So how does one heal such deep wounds of the soul?

Putting on the Armor: Agnes Sanford shares a prayer for battling against soul wounds in which I find remarkable power. I can find no better words than those lovingly expressed by this lady and wish to share with you this prayer (almost in its entirety). I recommend that in its utilization you offer it in its current form, or personalize the circumstances to better meet any particular situation for which you are praying.

This prayer can forge the shield with which those who suffer from a wounded soul can find strength and courage to resume their battles, both with the powers of this realm and with the true source of all spirit and soul wounds—the spiritual powers and authorities of evil within the spiritual realm.

There is an influx of intense energy when we begin to understand the need to forgive those who have caused us harm in order for internal healing to take place. And forgiveness is much easier to accomplish once we realize that the perpetrator's evil influence was orchestrated from spiritual forces of darkness, allowing us to let go of the anger, rage, and emotional outbursts toward the person, or people, involved in the conflict, and direct a determination toward the spiritual realm, wherein we will also find the strength for resolve.

❖ ❖ ❖

"Lord Jesus, I ask You to enter into this person who has need of your healing in the depths of the mind. I ask You to come, Lord, as a careful housekeeper might come into a house that has long been closed and neglected. Open all the windows and let in the fresh wind of Your Spirit. Raise all the shades, that the sunlight of Your Love may fill this house of the soul. Where there is sunlight there cannot be darkness. Therefore I rejoice that as the light of Your love now fills this mansion of the soul, all darkness shall flee away. And in deed in Your name I speak to that darkness, gently telling it that it cannot abide here in this one whom You have redeemed upon Your cross. Look and see, O Lord, whether there be any ugly pictures on the walls—pictures of old distressful and horrifying wounds of the past. And if there be such pictures, take them down and give to this memory-house pictures of beauty and joy. So out of all the ugliness of the past make beauty. O Lord, for it is ever Your nature to make beauty. Transform old sorrows into the power to comfort others who have sorrowed. Heal old wounds by Your redemptive love, and turn them mysteriously into a love that heals the wounds of others.

"Go back, O Lord, through all the rooms of this memory-house. Open every closed door and look into every closet and bureau drawer and see if there be any dirty and broken things that are no longer needed in

one's present life, and if so, O Lord, take them completely away. I give thanks, for this is the promise of the Scriptures: 'As far as the east is from the west, so far hath he removed our transgressions from us' (Psalms 13:12). Look, O Lord, upon any memories that come up from the deep mind as these words are meditated upon, and in Thy mercy fulfill in this Thy servant that forgiveness accomplished long ago on Calvary.

"Go back even to the nursery in this memory house—even to the years of childhood. Here, also, open windows long sealed and let in the gentle sunlight of Your love. Here more than anywhere, Lord, make everything clean and beautiful within. Take a broom of mercy and sweep away all dirt from the floor of this memory-room, even the confusion and the horror and shame of ancient memories, perhaps of childish and uncomprehended sins, perhaps of the sins of the parents, those parents who should have been as God Himself to the child and who were not. Take a clean cloth, O Lord, and wash away all dust and wipe away every stain from the walls and from the furniture. Purge this Your child with hyssop, O Lord, that the heart may be clean. Wash this one that the soul which is created in Your own image and after Your own likeness may be whiter than snow.

"Follow the soul of this Your child all the way back to the hour of birth and heal the soul even of the pain and the fear of being born into this darksome world. Restore in the soul that bright memory of Your eternal being that is not exactly a memory, but which is rather an emanation, an unconscious infilling of the eternal radiance from which this one was born. And if even before birth the soul was shadowed by this human life and was darkened by the fears or sorrows of the human parents, then I pray that even those memories or impressions may be healed, so that this one may be restored to Your original pattern, the soul as free and as clean as though nothing had ever dimmed its shining. Thus I pray, O Lord, that You will restore the soul as You made it to be and

will quicken and awaken in it all those creative impulses and ideas that
You have placed therein, so that whatever Your purpose may be for its
human pilgrimage, that purpose may be fulfilled.

"I give thanks, O Lord, knowing that this healing of the soul is Your will
and is the very purpose of the giving of Your life for us, and therefore it
is now being accomplished and by faith I set the seal upon it" (Sanford,
1982, pp.104–107).

❖ ❖ ❖

[Agnes Sanford was known as one of the leading Christian healing practitioners of the early 20th century. She was born in China as the daughter of a Presbyterian missionary, married an Episcopal Rector, and served faithfully in a healing ministry until her death].

Mrs. Sanford (1982) so rightly acknowledges that wounds of the soul which are not healed by self-searching and self-prayer "are inevitably connected with a subconscious awareness of sin, whether our own sin or our grievous reactions to the sins of others" (p. 110). "Whatever the issue, if it continues to hurt you, it probably remains incomplete and unhealed" (Walsh, 1999, p. 132).

With such deep and penetrating wounds, the patient must request the aid of a healer, or intermediary—someone to step in and pray with, and for, the individual. For sometimes we are too beaten to pray, sometimes we cannot forgive others, and sometimes we cannot forgive ourselves—forgiveness being the obvious place to start. Forgiveness might be equated to the action of putting on the belt of truth before tightening, because without forgiveness, the wisdom of truth will continue to evade us.

Though our unconscious mind (our spirit) may accept what needs to be done on our part, and the healing power available through forgiveness, our conscious mind may not. But when two or three join together in petitioning God to supply healing and forgiveness, our ability to take delivery of this gift can be ornately enhanced, and the forgiveness and healing of God can be received with absolution.

I liken this healing process to any healing process for the body, for, in fact, to create healing for the spirit or soul, we must first understand healing for their counterparts in the physical realm—the mind and body. As we examine the process for bringing healing to these physical entities, we then obtain a metaphor for which we can create healing for our spiritual entities. After praying a prayer like the one provided by Mrs. Sanford, it is time to go into battle. The following chart expresses this process.

Outline Comparing Physical Healing and Spiritual Healing

Physical Wounds	Soul Wounds
Evaluate the wound.	Examine its age/extent/depth.
Stop the bleeding—some bleeding is good.	When the soul bleeds, what comes out are expressions of emotions. Some emotions are good, but they must halt at some point for healing to occur.
Treat it with a healing agent—a trained person, medication, or ointment.	The healer must be one who understands the spirit/soul, not just a psychologist. Also go to the Creator of the soul through meditation and prayer.
Provide physical pain control through medication.	Provide spiritual pain control through spiritual counseling, meditation, and prayer.

Do not pick at the wound.	Do not continually bring up the matter in the mind — don't wallow in suffering.
Give the wound appropriate time to heal.	Allow for time in the healing process for the soul as well. Do not retaliate during the healing process: it will only delay healing.
Talk to the one who wounded you. Ask why, so you can move beyond the pain and fear.	Communicate with the oppressor. Determine if there is any personal fault — if so undo any damage you have done. If not, forgive and let go.
Work to help others avoid being hurt in the same way.	Helping others in the same situation brings purpose and meaning to one's life. It brings healing to self when we bring healing to others.

Spiritual leaders throughout history contend that the concept of kindness and service to others brings healing to the provider. With soul wounds, it is often the case that the patient has caused undue pain and suffering to others — often loved ones — in an ineffectual attempt to deal with personal pain. If we have harmed others in the past, we must begin our healing process with an additional step. We must communicate our sorrow to those we have harmed and we must vow to never harm again. Without this step in the process, we will not be able to move through the additional steps and healing will not occur for us. Many ancient spiritual writers extend this "no harm to others" to include any life-form within the creation. If so, we must not only make amends with people whom we have harmed, but with the universe at large.

If we are to be kind to others for the right reasons; if we are to desire to do no harm to all of the creation; if we are to live our life healed of our soul wounds; if we are to grow spiritually and to become enlightened; we must first deal with our past. For guilt, even unconscious guilt, will not allow for growth.

"Guilt-ridden people see their mistakes as unforgivable sins and punish themselves (or others) unmercifully. They do not heal or learn from the past. Ethical people recognize their mistakes as simply mistakes. They heal the past and themselves by correcting their error, forgiving themselves (and others), and learning as much as they can from the process" (Walsh, 1999, p. 136).

ASSERTION THREE

**We are each born with the key,
planted deep within our spirit,
to open the doorway which leads beyond the veil.**

**"But when you pray, go into your inner room, close
your door and pray to your [spiritual] Father who is
in secret, and your [spiritual] Father who sees what is
done in secret will reward you." (NASB, 1995).**

❖ ❖ ❖

[These are the words of the Anointed One, Christ, spoken during His ministry on this earth and written down for us around A.D. 70 by one of his personally chosen students, the apostle Matthew—Matthew 6:6].

This secret place into which we are to go and close the door is not a room in our house, but the inner room of our heart. It is the place where the personal key to our life is concealed—a point deep within our secret essence where the mind and spirit join forces in communicating with our Creator. It is in this place that answers can be found, intercessions can be made, and the sacred can be manifested. The door to our secret room opens the way to the spiritual realm. Our spirit, from within this sacred chamber, is the holder of the key and the only one who can unlock the door. How then do we locate our secret room—our sacred place? How do we connect with our spirit and gain access into the realm of the spiritual? How does our spirit, once touched by the Spirit of our Creator, reflect that light upon our physical being—our mind and body? *Through ritual!*

Ritual

Ritual is the pathway to the sacred—the means of transport en route to our spirit. Ritual brings spiritual energy to the physical. It opens windows to enlighten our entire being.

Ritual is also the formula utilized for centuries to guide students in the art of perseverance. It is patience in motion. It is a process which brings determined consistency and meaning to our daily tasks.

Ritual, in its physical form, is symbolic action with specific intent. It utilizes physical symbols to represent spiritual principles. Ritual takes us beyond opposites and introduces us to the *Principle of Similars.* "One must go beyond the pairs of opposites to find the real source" (Joseph Campbell as selected in Osbon, 1991, p. 200).

It is in the midst of ritualistic activity that our spirit feels most at home with our mind, our soul most at home with our body. From the moment of conception, our spirit is on a journey homeward, desperately wishing to guide our mind and body on the journey. Children, as the newfound offspring of the breath of God, are wonderful receptors of this spiritual energy, but seldom know how to channel it. Then, as adults, we lose the connection and must learn how to re-enter our secret place in order to reconnect with our spirit.

I am convinced that ritual is the only "physical" methodology in which the weakness of man's will can be overcome. Whether our goal and desire is developing patience, losing weight, becoming fit, discontinuing a negative habit, or getting closer to our Creator, through ritual, an ordinary activity becomes sacred. Once an ordinary activity becomes sacred, it becomes spirit-ritual. And as spirit-ritual, the spirit and soul lend their persuasive influence, encouraging the participant to persevere.

Joseph Campbell loved to visit magnificently designed cathedrals, seeing them as grand representatives of ritualistic power: "the symbolic details reflect, indeed, a local material history and environment, yet they are in an order of the mind, and to be interpreted by the faculty of reason as expressions of spiritual insight" (Joseph Campbell as selected in Osbon, 1991, p. 255). Once something becomes a truly ritualistic component of our lives, we will continue to find meaning in the activity and will patiently pursue it into eternity.

The mistake often made with ritual is that we pursue it simply as a physical endeavor. And if we do, somehow, perceive the spiritual implications, we often view them merely as metaphors, not as actual conduits for spiritual energy. Along with this misapplication in our action, we also tend to place the power of ritual in the exact replication of an activity, or in the implements utilized in the activity. With authentic ritual the power is not solely located in the activity or the implement, rather the ritual receives its power through the unique receptiveness of the individual in connecting with spiritual energy. In fact, throughout history, rituals are seldom passed on in a state of absolution because of their sacredness. It is through the personalization of a ritual that real meaning and power is brought to the participant—it must be adapted and molded to uniquely identify with each human spirit.

However, this does not bestow the authority to physically pervert a prescribed sacred ritual, but what it does is place a responsibility on the partaker to connect with the essence of the ritual, while complying with any God-given restraints. Nadab and Abihu, the priestly sons of the Israelite, Aaron, are perfect examples of perverting a prescribed ritual. When making a sacrificial animal offering, they were directed by God to only use a specific sacred fire. Instead, they offered a "strange fire" and were consumed therein (NASB, 1995, Leviticus 8:10). [The book of Leviticus provides laws and regulations for the worship and ritualistic activities of the people of Israel. It was written by Moses between 1446-1406 B.C. Moses was hand-selected by God to guide the Israelite people out of slavery and into a sacred land which God had set apart specifically for them].

So how do we connect with the essence of a ritual? How do we personalize, without perverting? How do we transform a simple ritualistic format into transformative power? Through the process of spirit-ritual!

Spirit-Ritual

The word spirit-ritual is derived from the word spiritual and is the most accurate translation of the action necessary to guide one toward spirituality. For within this simple word, *spiritual*, are two complete expressions: spirit and ritual (*spirit*ual/spi*ritual*.) It is the concept of our spirit connecting with our mind through ritual. Thus, it allows the mind to travel with the spirit on its metaphysical journey. But in order for a simple ritual to become a spirit-ritual, certain actions must first take place on a physical level. Our mind and body must prepare for the connection. But how?

1. We must first learn about the underlying purpose for the ritual, concentrating more on the purpose than the form. Although every spiritual movement has its rituals, many forms of conventional religion have lost the spirit of the ritual by inappropriately emphasizing the form. While tradition and ritualistic form can have immense meaning and purpose, without a knowledge and understanding of that purpose, the actions of the ritual fall on mute spirits and deaf minds. Without the necessary comprehension, a ritual can actually block our path on the road toward spiritual enlightenment.

2. We must personalize the ritual so that spiritual connections can be made between our mind and our spirit, allowing us to participate in the ritual from the spirit—not simply as a physical exercise of powerless routine. Practicing ritual, therefore, is not an exact formula, rather a uniquely idiosyncratic process.

3. We must begin the ritual with ceremonial preparation. In this fast-pace world in which we live, we often evade this stage and fail to take one of the most important steps in the ritualistic process. To bypass ceremonial preparation is like taking an unconditioned body and going forth to run a marathon. When the body is first readied for the activity, be it an exercise or a ritual, it can more appropriately take part in, and receive benefits from, the activity. Through ceremonial preparation, the body is conditioned to encounter the soul. Likewise, when the mind is made ready, it is more equipped to receive the activity, or ritual, and more apt to engage the spirit. Ritual teaches us the patience we need to be still—and in our stillness we connect, encounter, and engage.

4. We must learn about the meaning of the implements utilized in the ritual. Is there power generated through specific elements (stone, water, smoke, a plant, a drum, a symbol, a prayer formula, or the contents of a medicine bag, etc.). Or, are these items simply physical purification or encountering symbols, which can be interchangeably used for spiritual cleansing or spiritual connection *(Principle of Similars)*. In my studies of various Native American tribes I have found that it is often not *how* they danced, but *why* they danced. Not so much *which* sacred elements were used, but *that* sacred elements were used.

5. If mediators or healers are involved, we must investigate their character. We must be confident in their ability to be utilized as a purified vessel through which healing energy may flow. Pure energy cannot flow though an impure vessel.

6. We must investigate ourselves, or the ritual recipient, as to attitude, belief, willingness and preparedness to receive, whether it be healing, guidance, or affirmation. It is not so much the power of the ritual, but the readiness of the participant to connect and receive.

7. Foremost, we must invite our Creator to approve the purpose and the methodology; to cleanse and prepare the participants; and to empower the activity, the elements, and those partaking in the ritual. We must be careful, as well, to examine any God ordained plan of action for a prescribed ritual, so we do not pervert that which is already sacred.

8. And, finally, we must present sacrificial offerings of thanksgiving to the Creator, in acknowledgement that He is The Giver of All Things Good. And we must offer appreciation to those who took part in the ritualistic process.

When these eight principals are appropriately addressed, there can be true power exhibited through, and in, a spirit-ritual. Not just a representation of power, but true spiritual power as the activity, elements, and partakers are metaphysically energized by the Source of All Power.

Sometimes the physical symbols in ritual are simply utilized to teach us about the spiritual features. But at other times aspects of the physical are used to *present* the spiritual—spiritual power is actually channeled through physical properties and elements. Man is a perfect example of this channeling process: through mankind the Creator can present Himself and His healing/cleansing power to the world (touch, words, action, love, forgiveness, grace, mercy).

Likewise, the Creator of All Living Things can present Himself through elements of His creation. "There are things about God that people cannot see—His eternal power and all the things that make Him God. But since the beginning of the world those things have been easy for people to understand. Those things are made clear in the things God has made" (Holy Bible, Easy to Read Version, 2000—Romans 1:20).

Just as God's Spirit can come into our life and teach and energize our spirit—transform our spirit so that it can transform our physical constituents (mind and body)—God can energize the spirits within His creation so that they can be used as spiritual elements to transform other physical constituents (plants for healing, water for ceremonial cleansing or baptism, smoke as the transport of prayers). Our role, through ritual, is to prepare to receive the power, the energy, the message—to become appropriate receptors and transports for that which is sacred, to become cleansed vessels.

How then might we prove the existence of this power and its source? On a physical level, we cannot. For the power of the spiritual is formulated in the bonds of faith—"if a spiritual power could be proved it would lose its power, because the power comes from faith" (Sanford, 1983, p. 159). However, on a spiritual level, we *can* prove the existence of God and His power, but that truth is appropriated to our individual spirits. Man who looks to his spirit for answers, will find them. Man who looks only to science and the realm of the physical, will not.

What, then, is the methodology for transforming ritual into spirit-ritual? One must examine each ritual within which one participates, against the eight noted components necessary for authentic spirit-ritual.

The Spirit-Ritual of Sex:

Why would I begin with such a physical act as sex for an example of spirit-ritual? Because sex, in its sacred form, provides a perfect illustration of how all rituals are to be prepared and performed.

Sex, like any ritual, can be performed simply as a *physical act* of pleasure and self-satisfaction. It can be performed as a *physical ritual*, but without spiritual meaning or purpose. Or it can be performed as a *spirit-ritual*, with deep spiritual implications.

As a spirit-ritual, the concept of sex begins with an understanding of the purpose for sex. Sex is not meant to be exploited as a mere recreational activity. For it is not only the union of two bodies, but as understood within the *Principle of Opposites*, it is the union of two souls—two bodies cannot be joined together without the union of their opposites. And the union of souls is a matter of serious and eternal consequences.

As a spirit-ritual, in step two, *the act of sex must be uniquely personalized for those participating.* A knowledge must be acquired of each other's body, but also of each other's mind. With knowledge of the body, comes an understanding of the soul; with knowledge of the mind, an understanding of the spirit. One should never have sex without first developing an intimate knowledge and understanding of the other person.

Next, as noted in step three: *When the body is first readied for the activity, be it an exercise or a ritual, it can more appropriately take part in, and receive benefits from, the activity. Through ceremonial preparation, the body is conditioned to encounter the soul. Likewise, when the mind is made ready, it is more equipped to receive the activity, or ritual, and more apt to engage the spirit.* Ceremonial preparation is the key element. For sexual activity, this preparation might include: taking a shower, putting on perfume or cologne, listening to music, sharing soft looks and kind words, dinner, loving touch, kissing, gentle teasing, or other types of ritualistic foreplay. Ritual teaches us the patience we need to be still — and in our stillness we connect, encounter, and engage.

Step four: *we must learn about the meaning of the implements utilized in the ritual.* Obviously the implements utilized in sexual activity are the bodies, including the penis and vagina. But much too often these "body parts" are considered the primary objects of the sexual experience, and too little emphasis is placed on the mind, the spirit, and the soul. Continuing with the previous Native American example, I have found that it is often not *how* they had sex, but *why* they had sex. Not so much *which* parts of the body were used, but *that* the parts of the body were used in a sacred manner and that the experience involved the *whole* person.

Step five: if we look to someone for sexual advice and healing, be it a professional counselor or friend, *pure energy cannot be channeled through an impure vessel.* Choose wisely those from whom you ask for guidance and direction.

Step six: *we must investigate ourselves, and the ritual recipient, as to attitude, belief, willingness and preparedness to participate. For it is not so much the power of the ritual, but the readiness of the participant to connect and receive.* One should never take part in sexual activity until they are spiritually mature enough to do so in a sacred manner, with an understanding of the significance of the action and of the potential consequences.

Step seven: *we must be careful to examine any God ordained plan of action for a prescribed ritual so we do not pervert that which is already sacred.* Sex, as a spirit-ritual, is meant to take place only between two committed, married individuals.

And finally, step eight: *we must be thankful to God for the blessing of sex and find ways to show our sexual partner that we appreciate the intimacy shared through the act of sex.* Part of this appreciation can be shown by lying still together, caressing, slowly untangling, or going to sleep in each other's arms after sex.

When the act of sex becomes a spirit-ritual, it opens the doorway to true intimacy. It opens the doorway to the spiritual realm. It becomes sacred-sex.

The Spirit-Ritual of the Spirit-Candle:

The second ritual I discuss is one which helps the participant connect with the inner-spirit and better understand how this connection takes place. Choose a candle with purpose — one which seems to speak to you. Light the candle and place it several feet away from you in a darkened, tranquil room. Relax as you begin to look at the candle. Allow your muscles to sink toward the floor. As you breathe in — slow deep breaths — imagine the candle flame sharing its energy with your mind. As you breathe out, imagine your mind sharing its energy with the flame. Repeat this process for ten to fifteen minutes, or until you feel your mind and the candle flame are one.

The flame represents your spirit, and as you become one with the flame, you become one with your spirit. You become in-spirit. Other similar processes of becoming one through meditation can greatly assist in shutting out the clutter of the world and discovering that place where you become in-spirit. Once in-spirit, you can share your spirit with others by imagining those you wish to "touch." With their image in mind/spirit, breathe in and draw on their energy. Then breath out, sharing your energy—your spirit.

The touch of a shared-spirit has been described as the sensation of a feather passing near the skin. A stronger spirit-field has been described as the warmth and peace of a loving embrace; it is personal knowledge of another's presence, though they are not physically present.

In the spirit-candle ritual one can also work to manipulate the flame, but will find that it cannot be done with force, rather it must be accomplished with a gentle union of spirit and mind. With practice, we can learn to leave our image, or our spirit-imprint, in something we make, with someone we meet, in a house, or in other places we have been—Oh, if these walls could but talk!

The Spirit-Ritual of Prayer:

The early Cherokee were said to have danced in prayer. A powerful dance included people of like-mind, united in spirit, soul, mind, and body, becoming one source of united prayer to God. Such a prayer was believed to be stronger than any audible words. The united response of many becoming one holds the power of "touching" the Creator in a way that individual prayer cannot. The words, the thoughts, the emotions, the actions, leave the single entity and converge with the words, thoughts, emotions, and actions of the many. Together they travel upward beyond the veil, rising as a sweet sound before the One Who Created Sound by His words—and He responds.

But one might say, an all-knowing God implies one who comprehends our needs, even before we ask. Why then should we pray? Through prayer, we build a bridge of unity between the spiritual and the physical. When we pray, it is not only us communicating with our Creator, but it also opens us up as receptors for communication *from* God. Think about talking with a friend and then listening for a response. If we do not talk to our friend, he cannot respond. Through our communication process, we begin to hear and better understand each other. In prayer, we are asking God to be involved in our lives, and we, in turn, are becoming involved in His. We are asking for unity between the realm of the physical and the spiritual. Our Creator will never force His way upon us; therefore, we must anxiously employ Him to participate in our daily mission.

A common mistake we make, though, is that we pray for something, but we do not listen for a response. We pray, then go about our business without allowing the opportunity for a response to be received by our spirit, much less allowing for the mind to comprehend the spirit. And then we complain that our prayers are not answered. Always allow a time of patient-waiting after a time of prayer. If we ask someone for an answer, but do not listen for the response, we cannot expect to benefit from his or her gifts. It is the same with our Creator. It is not so much that He does not respond; it is more often that we do not listen. And if we do listen, it is with our physical mind, which is seldom in concert with our spirit.

True, effective prayer must take place on a spiritual level—we must pray in-spirit. This is where authentic belief takes place. Likewise, when we learn to pray in-spirit, and believe in-spirit, we will be granted answers to our prayers in-spirit. For the laws of the spirit and soul are not the same as the laws of the body—they are not subject to the same restraints. Forgiveness, healing, direction, guidance, and all other spiritual blessings are first received in-spirit; they initially take place on a spiritual plane. We must then provide a suitable metaphysical channel through which transfer can take place. It is only through the stability of this intrinsic energy that our spiritual answers can be manifested on a physical plane. If we are not receiving physical manifestations of our spiritual requests, we have not yet perfected oneness of our spirit, soul, mind, and body—a degree of harmony necessary for blessings from above to be made evident below.

Through the avenue of prayer, we utilize aspects of our physical existence to enter the realm of the spirit. We begin with the mind but pass through and enter the spirit; we pass through the body and enter the soul. By means of the unconscious mind, we pass from one to the other. We learn from the physical ritual of prayer how to connect with and address the spiritual. Once within the spiritual realm, we obtain and bring back answers as to how to address the physical.

But for what should we pray, and for whom should we pray? Our prayers may follow a variety of *formulas*, but for the most part they can be identified within these categories: *petitions for our personal wants, needs, and desires; petitions for the wants, needs, and desires of others; offerings of forgiveness; requests for forgiveness; offerings of thankfulness and praise; appeals for deliverance from evil; pleas for peace; pleas for strength in our earthly struggles; and requests for guidance, direction, and answers to life's daily and eternal questions.* Through these *prayers of faith* we create intimacy between man and God, keep the doors of physical/meta-physical communication open, and unlock pathways for the transfer of spiritual energy.

And for whom shall we pray—for we cannot pray for everyone. We should pray for those whose names are placed upon our hearts. As we open the doors of prayer-communication, those who need our prayers will be made know to us.

Prayer formulas and mantras: Prayer formulas and mantras are a part of both eastern and western spiritual movements. They each place a power in the words spoken and the state of mind of the speaker. Common formulas include: developing an individualized ritual for personal prayer preparation—going through a personalized routine before entering into prayer; determining to whom one will pray—typical prayers are directed to God, Heavenly Father, or Creator; naming or listing the names of those whom one wishes to be affected by the prayers; visualizing the action of the prayer taking place; letting others see you pray as a means of witness and confirmation, but also directing some prayers in solitude; and praying for others first, self last.

The Cherokee people are keepers of some of the best known prayer formulas—formulas for everything from healing, love, self-protection, hunting, or causing another person harm. The Swimmer, Gatigwanasti, Gahuni, and Inali Manuscripts, all noted within James Mooney's *Sacred Formulas of the Cherokees*, are a treasure chest of such historical data collected from the Cherokee Indian Reservation in North Carolina from 1887-1888. Though many of these formulas are difficult for the non-Indian (and often the Indian as well) to decipher, the message of purpose is consistently documented as "power in the spoken word, especially ritualistically chosen words and words which address the influx of spiritual power" (Mooney, 1891). [The anthropologist and writer, James Mooney, lived many years among the Cherokee people and is responsible for a sizeable amount of data relating to Cherokee lifestyle and rituals. Most of his research was conducted during his career and through his publications while with the Bureau of American Ethnology].

A prayer formula, or mantra, will often be a simple set of words repeated over and over until the mind and body accept what the spirit desires. They may be words to calm: *Oh Lord, give me peace.* Words of encouragement: *Through you, oh God, I can do all things.* Or words for purification: *Cleanse me Creator and make me whole.* By repeating these phrases, and believing them, their spiritual energy is transferred from a metaphysical level to a physical level, and peace appears, confidence builds, and cleansing occurs.

Prayers for our personal wants, needs, and desires: "You don't get the things you want because you don't ask God. Or when you ask, you don't receive. Why? Because the reason you ask is wrong. You only want things so that you can use those things for your own pleasures (Holy Bible, Easy to Read Version, James 4: 2-3). What is important in the mind of the one praying — relationships to people, or relationships to things? Are things more important than a strong rapport with God, more important than a growing relationship with others? Is getting what is personally desired more important than others getting what they need and want? There is nothing wrong in asking our Maker and Creator to bless our life, and He will gladly do so, but our mind must not be self-seeking, or our prayers will go unfilled. Seek first for God to fulfill the needs of others, and in so-seeking you shall also find comfort for self.

Pray a prayer and do not ask for anything for self. See how difficult this proves to be. When you slip and ask for something for self (and you will), gently guide your mind and spirit back to another's needs.

Prayers of forgiveness: We must become pure vessels in order for spiritual energy to work through us — we must be forgiven and our spirits seek this forgiveness. We must ask for this forgiveness from those we have harmed. If we cannot reach those we have harmed, our spirits find it meaningful to share our wrongs with those in whom we trust, and with our Creator who has the power to not only forgive but to forget - to wipe clean our slate. Likewise, we cannot become pure vessels if there are those for whom we hold resentment. We must be forgiving in order to be forgiven, and we must be a forgiving people to make a way for spiritual power to enter us. A spirit and mind which hold anger and resentment have no room left for spiritual energy. A helpful ritual is to make a note of those whom you have harmed, cheated, spoken against, etc. Then write, call, or go visit these people, and in so doing, cleanse your soul.

ASSERTION THREE

Before taking part in any ritual, pray for forgiveness and for the gift of a forgiving spirit.

Prayers of daily thankfulness and praise: "Whenever we pray for something and receive it, one thing that our people are taught to do is say thank you. When you do that, many more blessings come" (Bear Heart, 1998 p.95). We must be a thankful people, for when we do not show appreciation for our blessings, our blessings diminish. Set aside a period of time, or a prayer, where you only impart thankfulness — no requests, no questions, no self-seeking, only thankfulness.

For this reason, each day as I arise, I give thanks for something that has meaning in my life. It may be the simple warmth of the heater, the beauty of the deer in the front yard, my family, my job, my morning cup of tea, the sunshine, or the rain. The important thing is to find ways to offer thanks every day, and in turn, you will find more meaning in each day.

Prayers or grace before a meal: "Ritual introduces you to the meaning of what's going on. Saying grace before meals lets you know that you're about to eat something that once was alive" (Campbell, Joseph, as selected in Osbon, Diane K., 1991, p.90). But I am a vegetarian, one might say. To which Campbell might reply: all of creation is living, the vegetarian is simply one who eats that which cannot run away.

Traditional Native American tribes follow this same line of thought. Before taking the life of an animal, the native hunter will ask the spirit of the animal to freely give of its life in order to sustain the life of the hunter. To not offer this prayer is believed to result in physical suffering for the hunter. Likewise, an Indian gatherer of herbs and plants will offer prayers before taking his bounty, and will procure no more than needed.

Jewish tradition embraces prayer before all meals. In fact, to eat or drink without offering a prayer, or asking a blessing over the meal, is considered robbing from the Creator, the One from whom all sacred blessings flow, and the One from whom all blessings may cease to flow, as well (Smith,

1991). [Huston Smith is one of the best known modern authorities on the history of religions. He has been a professor at Washington University, MIT, Syracuse University, and University of California at Berkeley].

A prayer or grace over food and drink should ask the Creator to infuse the sustenance with energy, so that it may empower the one partaking with the strength needed to go out and work to serve others—that the food will be used as an energy source and not to be stored as excess fat. The one praying should also thank the Creator and all those responsible for bringing the food to his table. It helps to imagine the farmer planting the seed and harvesting the crop, the truck driver bringing the product to market, and the grocery store clerk cleaning and preparing the food, then placing it on the shelf for you to purchase.

Prayers for deliverance from evil: (see *The Spirit-Ritual of Removing the Presence of Evil*).

Prayers for peace: We must be people of peace in order to pray for peace. In order to be a people of peace we must: be under the authority of rulers and government—obeying them in things that are not evil; speak no evil about another person; keep peaceful relationships with each person with whom we come in contact; be gentle in word and deed; show kindness and politeness to all people; not be slaves to our own selfish desires; and stay away from those who are trouble makers and arguers (Titus 3:1-3 & 9). [Taken from the words of the Apostle Paul around A.D. 64 to his friend, co-worker, and travel partner, Titus].

One who truly seeks peace will find it, even in the midst of turmoil. For while an outward environment of peace is often generated by the outward deeds of many, a true peace is a quality generated from within the individual spirit. A prayer ritual for peace should first ask the Creator for the guidance to create an external environment in which peace will flourish, while also asking for the inner strength to relinquish the requirement for external peace to be present as a prerequisite for inner-peace.

Prayers for strength in our earthly struggles: There are two approaches to life: life is difficult, so get used to it; life is neither difficult nor easy, rather it is our approach to life which makes it hard. Which is true?

By accepting life as hard, are we able to change our approach to life and thereby reduce life's frustrations? Or do we, by accepting, claim defeat and enter a survivalist mode of living? On the other hand, if we see life as neither easy nor hard, are we simply viewing life romantically? Or, does this approach allow us the wisdom to make wise choices and avoid many of life's irritations?

Maybe, just maybe, both of these approaches hold truth, and it is we who choose our approach based on our environment and training. As I ask my friends the approach they accept, most acknowledge "life is difficult." To me, this is very sad, yet I find it easy to get drawn into this attitude of disappointment because of the environmental vibrations which surround me. I, however, when apart from this negative environment, acknowledge "life is neither easy nor hard." Life is life; it is our approach which makes it difficult or easy. The way we live is a personal choice. Do we merely survive and allow everything to be hard, or do we rebel against this standard approach and live with enthusiasm and energy—taking the good with the bad, but not expecting it to be bad, and definitely not coercing it to be bad in a self-fulfilling prophecy.

Does my view make me a romantic at heart? Yes! And while those around me strive to make life hard, I will strive to make life full. How, then, can this view be reflected in an everyday prayer life? We pray from our present frame of mind, and our spirit is thus transformed. If we pray from a survivalist frame of mind, we will receive exactly what we believe we will receive, which is pain and suffering. But, if we can change our mind and follow our spirit, we can pray with confidence, with a belief that life is what we make of it—that life is good.

Then, for what should we pray in order to make this change of heart? Our relationships, our jobs, our personal stressors, the aging of our physical bodies and minds, physical sickness, death, difficulties with love, our toil in striving to do and be good, and our day-to-day struggles. Pray not that these items will all be eliminated, but that they may be appreciated. This list of items, more than any others, are the ones repeatedly noted by my students and clients as those areas which make life hard—yet each of these items is an intricate part of the fabric of life. Pray that these areas of your life will be transformed by a romantic spirit of optimism and see your stressors become *challenges* and your hardships become *opportunities for growth.*

Prayers for guidance, direction, and answers: Where do we look for answers to life's questions? From whom do we seek guidance and direction? Unfortunately, there are few mortal men qualified to mentor us on this spiritual quest, yet mortal men we seek through an enormous array of spiritual books and counselors.

Not to say that these books and counselors cannot assist with our journey, but our questions for guidance and direction for life should first be presented to our Creator. In-spirit we can connect with the Source of our existence and find meaning. This meaning is not reserved for decisions of immense proportions; it is available for the minutest of our daily tasks. But, we must ask, and we must do so with confidence in the Source of supply and a willingness to surrender our will to the will of our Maker. For often we ask, but seldom we abide.

Set aside a time to be still with God, to center your entire attention on Him, and to pray for guidance, direction, and answers to anything upon your mind. Then listen, not simply with your mind, but with your spirit. Then, in-spirit, follow the path provided with boldness. By asking our Creator to oversee our journey in all things, we can better distinguish truth from error, selfish desires from selfless desires, and an honest path from the way of deceit.

Prayers of faith: The prayer of faith is exactly what it implies, a prayer uttered with purpose and confidence. "The prayer that is said with faith will make the sick person well. The Lord will heal that person" (Holy Bible, Easy to Read Version, 2000, James 5:15). "Apparently the prayer of faith makes a channel between God and the sick person, so that the Lord can raise him up. This prayer is quite simply just what it says: a prayer of faith, not a prayer of worship or a prayer of contemplation, valuable though they are. Nor is it a prayer of vain repetitions, of beseeching, though that too has its place. The prayer of faith calmly and quietly asks for a specific thing and then sends forth the word of power, either saying, 'Let it be so,' which is the literal translation of the word 'Amen,' or saying in more simple words, as I am apt to do: Thank you, Lord. I believe that your power is entering into this person, working toward the wholeness that I see in my mind, Amen" (Sanford, 1983, pp. 164-165).

Mrs. Sanford (1982) provides a four fold spirit-ritual in successfully praying this prayer of faith.

1. Choose a specific symptom or weakness for which to pray — don't try to pray for everything at once.

2. Use healing words which suggest to the body positive reinforcement and a cure, rather than negatively reinforcing the trials and torments of the patient. And use strong words of faith such as "according to your will," rather than words of weakness, such as "if it be your will."

3. Visualize in your mind a positive answer to the prayer.

4. Thank God for His power in honoring your request, even before you experience His answer.

For is not "all prayer, in essence, an attempt to work out and establish what we believe to be God's will" (p. 48-51)? So, then, is it not only good, but imperative, that we seek healing through prayers of faith for those who are sick, praying with all confidence, yet leaving the methodology of healing up to God and His will.

Cherokee healing also consists of "a prayer of faith," believing that the combination of appropriate action and prayers of faith, by the healer *and* the one being healed, are essential in order for healing to occur. Both parties must believe that the patient will either be cured, or that there is a vital, spiritual reason why healing should not occur (Mails, 1988, p. 120). [Thomas Mails is one of the most renowned modern American researchers dealing with the ethnology of Native Americans. His style is to study and compare their past and present lifestyles, rituals, governing systems, and beliefs. He is a retired Lutheran minister from California].

The Spirit-Ritual for Removing the Presence of Evil:
Are there evil forces which still influence the ways of man? Where do these evil forces come from? In what manner can these evil forces present themselves? And what can we do to protect ourselves, or rid ourselves and others, from such evil?

In response to question one and two, there seems to be no reservation, on the part of any of the spiritual movements under study, that evil does exist and still has an influence on mankind today. It also appears that evil has been in existence since the earliest of recorded time. Western religions assert that mankind invited evil into the world, in the beginning, and still lays out the welcome mat today.

In the Judeo-Christian story of creation, God placed a tree, containing knowledge about good and its opposite evil, within the sacred garden in which His new creation dwelt. God did not create the evil, but as "All Knowing" was aware of its potentiality because of the manner of His creation. Not wishing to force the way of the Creator upon the creation, God made His creation to have free choice—choice to follow after peace and the way of the Master, or freedom to follow the way of desire.

Satan (a fallen, created angel who had already made his self-seeking choice), seeing his opportunity to tempt the desires of the new creation, invited himself first into the being of a snake and then into the life of mankind, forever. This fallen angel knew first-hand what desire could do to a creation with freewill, so he asked the woman, then the man, to welcome evil into the world under the mask of Godly knowledge. The desires of mankind did not resist, and knowledge was the gift, but with the gift came the pain. And with the pain, death.

Since that time, evil has lived alongside good and will continue doing so until the end of the physical world as we know it. The creation, both good and bad, man and animal, plant and soil, water and air, will suffer the consequences.

Question Three: In what ways can these evil forces present themselves? The following are means identified within many religious or spiritual movements in which evil makes itself known.

Man's Evil Influence:
- We can *become* evil by following selfish desires—jealousy and selfishness are often listed as the apex of human desires.
- We can *create* evil by following selfish desires, and this evil can then influence self and others.
- Others near us can influence us with their evil.
- Those far away can influence us with their evil—wars, abuse, etc.

Evil Spirits' Influence:
- Spirits exist in the cosmos.
- Man's spirit can become evil while alive and create disorder..
- Man's spirit can remain evil after death; some believe this spirit can then come back, or remain on the earth, causing havoc.

- There are created beings, both good and those who have chosen evil; some believe these evil spirits can cross the veil and cause discord on the earth.

Indwelling of Evil Spirits:
- Within the recorded history of many of the various religions are documented evidence of extra-earthly spirits entering human or other life forms and taking control of their capacities.

Question four: What can we do to protect ourselves, or rid ourselves, from such evil? There emerges a very common formula from the western religions, with many of the principles also common among eastern religions.
- Self Purification
- Pray with force, power, and the influence of good for the evil to leave
- Believe in what is being prayed for
- Put the evil in the hands of the Creator of all things
- Rebuke the evil to never return—that it has no acceptable place in your life
- Pray for the space the evil occupied to be filled by God and a spirit of good
- Thank God, praise God, for fulfilling the request
- Ask for guidance and safety in future service and in helping others rid themselves of the presence of evil.

If the evil is of a personal nature, or resides within someone close, the ritual begins with self purification. Among various groups this purification includes: smudging with smoke, a sweat lodge ceremony, water purification, and prayer. Each ceremony is directed toward preparing the participant to become an active partaker in the ritual of removing the presence of evil. Purification involves a self examination of the participant, asking the Creator to forgive and cleanse any wrong or evil within, and asking for protection from the influence created by the evil during the entire process.

After purification, the participant prays with force and power for the evil to leave—not a force and power from within the physical self, but a request to be used as a vessel through which the power of God can make itself manifest. Within the Christian faith, the believer will pray through the power and name of Jesus, the Christ, the Anointed One, "commanding" the evil to be gone. I have know those who tried too hard to *be* the source of power themselves and in so doing were unable to see their request come to fruition. And even though one might request for evil to be cast out of self, I have encountered those so weakened by the source of evil that it was necessary for someone else to make the prayer request on their behalf.

Only prayers of faith can be effective against such forces as evil, so the participant must believe in what is being prayed for. Jesus gave this advice: "All things for which you pray and ask, believe that you *have* received them, and they will be granted you" (NASB, 1999, Mark 11:24 [italics added]). The term "have" implies the request should be visualized before actual completion of the appeal. One is to believe that an answer to the petition has already occurred, not that it will or may occur in the future. Seeing our prayers answered in our mind and spirit is a form of faith in action, thereby strengthening the request.

Man does not have the ability, or knowledge, of what should be done with evil, so he is to put it in the hands of the Creator of all things before they became evil. The Creator determines whether or not to destroy the evil.

It is then a time to tell the evil which has been removed to never return, for if there is power to remove the evil, that same power can also keep it far away.

It is said that man often rids himself of something negative, only to replace it with something worse. In rituals to remove evil, there are typically prayers for the space that the evil occupied to be consumed by God and a spirit of good. It is also said, among the western religions, that evil cannot exist in a being in whom the Spirit of God dwells—the two cannot co-exist in the same creature—thus, making the quest for God to dwell within the spirit of man, a focal point for a spiritual explorer. If all men, then, had the Spirit of God, evil would be conquered (see the *Ritual of Going to Water*).

All religions express the need to show appreciation for gifts granted, and in so doing, the participant is richly blessed. One is to thank God, praise God, for fulfilling the request. An ungrateful spirit is easily seized by desire.

And lastly, a common plea is a solicitation for future guidance and safety in serving and helping others eliminate the presence of evil. A universal deterrent to evil recognized by both eastern and western religions is sacred service. By continuing to do good, even in the face of evil, evil will be defeated.

Evil, be it evil influence or the presence of an evil spirit, constructs a dangerous pathway. One should never treat it lightly, always equipping oneself with power, from the Source of All Power, before ever attempting to eradicate its presence. For it is common, even for one of good intent, to be misdirected down an iniquitous trail as he is drawn away by his own evil desires.

There is a story of some Jewish exorcists attempting to cast out evil spirits around A.D. 63. These men were using the name of the Christ to adjure the spirits, but they themselves did not know and believe in the Christ. The evil spirit within one of their clients confronted them: "I recognize Jesus, and I know about Paul, but who are you?" The spirit then attacked the exorcists (NASB, 1999, Acts 19:13-14). The message for one attempting to cast out evil? Know the Source of the power before you attempt to utilize its energy.

The Spirit-Ritual of Worship:

Within the United States the largest formal worship system is the one surrounding Christianity, but within this overall format is a multiplicity of configurations. And, regrettably, many of today's worship styles leave much to be desired. Worship has become something we *do*; church has become somewhere we *go*. Yet, we go and do and by our goings and doings are little affected. We go and do without meaning or purpose; instead, we go and do simply as a social obligation or misunderstood responsibility. Worship was never intended to be an institutionalized compulsion. It was, and is to be, a very personal, functional communication process between Creator and creation. Worship should always begin on a private level, and any social or formal attachment is to be one for the sharing of common bonds and edification of spirit and mind. This does not mean that formal worship is spiritually unprofitable, but formal worship without private practice neglects its primary purpose.

"If you can't get into yourself on the level of the Christ within you, you are not a Christian. And depending on the level of awareness you have reached, your worship will be different from that of people in the same church who aren't at the same level. Saying you are a member of this church, that church, or the other is a social notion, a sociological phenomenon that has nothing to do with religion" (Campbell, Joseph, as selected in Osbon, Diane K., 1991, p.204).

So how then should man worship? "God is Spirit and those who worship Him must worship in spirit and truth" (NASB, 1995, John 4:8). Man is, first, to worship in-spirit. We are not only to worship with our physical mind, but with our inner spirit. We have already spoken, in-depth, about the spiritual essence of all things created. It is with this essence (spirit) we should communicate with God.

And to worship "in truth" requires that the worshiper seek out authentic truth—another goal of the spiritual seeker. Our worship should change as we grow. As we find truth, we incorporate it in our worship. And as we worship in-spirit and in-truth, we connect beyond the veil and find even more truth. True worship is to be an ever-evolving process.

Throughout time, typical rituals utilized in worship among various eastern and western religions are: praying, singing, chanting, playing of musical instruments, dancing, sharing of words of praise and wisdom, offering, healing, performing commitment and communion ceremonies, fellowshipping, and meditating—most of which will be separately discussed in this section under the titles of specific rituals. Those not discussed as a specific ritual are: singing, chanting, and reciting words of praise and wisdom. These are discussed below.

"Speaking to one another in psalms and hymns and spiritual songs, singing and making melody with your heart to the Lord" (NASB, 1995, Ephesians 5:13). Think of the vibrations of sound lifting from the bodies of numerous singers and collecting in the air, then this breath of mankind, bonded together, traveling, not only to those around us, but to a higher plane—like smoke rising from a fire directed toward the heavens. If the words and thoughts are genuine, if they come from our inward being wishing to communicate with the Creator, if they come from our seeking after truth, they are spirit-song. And as they collect and travel through the veil, they carry with them our spirit. We have now worshiped in-spirit and in-truth through our song, our chant, or our words of praise and wisdom.

The benefit of such worship? Through regular, open, communication with our Creator, we not only praise Him, but are inwardly energized by His presence in the worship ceremony. By honoring the Source of power and blessings, the power and blessings more freely flow. Worship brings about wholeness and oneness with God.

The Spirit-Ritual for Creating a Sacred Place:

"The idea of a temple is what is here announced, an enclosure wherein every feature is metaphorical of a connoted metaphysical intuition, set apart for ritual enactments" (Campbell, Joseph, as selected in Osbon, Diane K., 1991, p.256). A sacred place is a physical space in which we, through ritual, connect with our Creator. It can be anywhere we choose or anywhere that chooses us: a church, a tepee, a room in our home, a sacred spot beneath a tree, a bolder in the middle of a river, a secluded cabin in the woods, or a mountain perch. What makes the place sacred is that we, individually and meticulously, seek it out and dedicate it as a place where we connect with God.

As I write this section I am in one of my sacred places, a small and secluded creek-side cabin just outside the Qualla Boundary, better known as the Cherokee Indian Reservation, North Carolina. It is a place without television and other mental distractions which tend to restrict spiritual union. A place in which I can simply "be"—in the past, present, or future, as desired.

When I first leased this cabin it had a satellite connection for a large television, which is now disconnected. At first, I mourned this loss like the passing of a friend, but I very quickly came to appreciate the quietness I had been missing at home. I now seek the solitude of this sacred place on a monthly basis. A place I can involve my mind and spirit in what I refer to as spirit-pondering—allowing my mind and spirit to unite and take me on a journey of meaningful thought and reflection.

For many of us our sacred place is a temple, church building, or synagogue, and if traditionally based these structures are either exceptionally elaborate in design or overtly simplistic in form, yet for a reason. These extreme opposites each provide unique spiritual inspiration in their radical differences. From the divinely created sunlight streaming through ornately hand-painted windows visited in Ireland, to the simple wooden pews and twirling ceiling fans in one of the historic churches in Cades Cove, we are touched by God. As we enter the door of either one of these places of worship we can *feel* the sounds, smells, and signs of its spiritual history.

In the 1970's we, unfortunately, became very dreary in our architectural design of sacred places. Our buildings became *neutral*—and neutral does not the spirit inspire. I am afraid we actually lost an entire generation of potential spirit-seekers through our creation of uninspiring places of worship. And only recently have we begun to correct this misguided error. With a return to simplistic form and grand elegance we will most certainly open new eyes to spiritual beauty.

While buildings of worship can become wonderful sacred places for our spirits to awaken, they are not *personal* sacred spaces. By creating a personal sacred place we meet an internal spiritual need that cannot be satisfied in any other way. But how do we locate such a site?

To establish a personal sacred place, we must find a setting that speaks to us, a place that inspires us, a place with few material distractions. Nature provides the grandest sacred places, as well as any piece of land which has been gifted to us, places that remind us of good days gone by, and old, *lived-in* structures. The location should be cleansed through prayer—Indians might include smudging. It should also be free from clutter, debris, and any man-made excess. The space should be comfortable, but not so relaxing that it always lures one to sleep. It should be a place full of spirit-life or representations of such—animals, plants, water, soil, stone, fresh air and light, fire, and naturally created sounds.

Many Native Americans will surround their sacred place with prayer ties (see *Offering Ritual: Blessings upon the Creation*). Sacred objects and symbols may be stored, and used, in one's sacred place—journals, Bibles, prayer books, candles, incense, and other items set apart for a higher purpose.

Most sacred places face the east—the home of the rising sun, symbolizing new beginnings—but this may be left to personal preference.

The most important aspects of a personal sacred place is that it inspires, is a place of individualized beauty in its simplicity or symbolic detail, and creates an environment in which we can communicate with our spirit and the Spirit of our Creator. We should all make finding such a place a priority in our spiritual journey.

The Spirit-Ritual for Healing:

"To become powerful is to allow a Greater Power to work through you. But seeking power just to be considered powerful—we don't even talk about it" (Bear Heart, 1998, p.81). Bear Heart maintains that a belief established within the patient is what initiates the healing process and that many of the steps taken by the healer are a deliberate intent to bring about this belief.

I strongly support Bear Heart's conviction. Is it not the patient who, within his corporal structure, already has the means for self-healing as prescribed by our Creator? And does not this power also indwell all of creation, wherewith her elements might also be called upon to assist with the procedure?

Secondly, the healer's own energy comes into account. The healer must also believe that a power exists which heals, and that he, indeed, has access to that power. Not that the power is his, but that he is an instrument through which healing may occur. The healer is then compelled to bring about a belief in the patient which is equal to his own. Much of any ritualistic action he imparts during a healing discourse is directed toward this end (Bear Heart, 1998, pp. 88-90).

Dr. Jung (1957) adds that the doctor or healer must "establish a relationship with both halves of his patient's personality" (p. 87). He must understand what is happening on a physical level, including the mental state of the patient, as well as on a spiritual level, before he can assist in the healing process. It is my belief that healing occurs first on the plain of the spiritual. It is then up to the patient to connect spirit with mind and soul with body in such a way that the effect of the spiritual healing is transferred upon the physical. This, likewise, reinforces my conviction that wounds of the soul have not been adequately dealt with on a spiritual level, and until this happens, no physical formula for recovery will suffice.

Agnes Sanford (1983) asserts that in the act of healing we must claim God's power to change the laws of probability or so-called fate. She strongly believes that as God can enter any part of His creation to construct and heal, He can also enter into His creation and destroy, anything from cancerous cells to negative emotions. Is not the power of the Creator stronger then that of fate?

Our Creator, then, has the power to enter into the creation and heal or enter into the creation and destroy. Most do not question this reality. Our query is more likely, how might we claim the presence of this power?

Mrs. Sanford also acknowledges that all diseases cannot, or will not, be healed within the earthly realm because many are not merely diseases of the individual, but diseases of the society in which we live. Until mankind works to heal the spiritual depravity of his mind and his environment, he will not be able to experience the total healing of his body. Likewise, if man continues to destroy his own body through the ways in which he lives, in his lack of exercise, poor diet, and negative habits, His God will not enter into him with healing energy. Man must be willing to change his ways in order to receive God's healing powers.

"Sioux healers have known for a long time what modern medicine is just now beginning to assert — that most all illness begins in the mind" (Mails, 1988, p. 221). Fools Crow, a ceremonial chief and medicine man of the Lakota Sioux and nephew of Black Elk, agrees. Fools Crow distinguishes between healing and curing by noting that all people die — so people cannot all be cured of physical ailments. But, on one level or another, all people can receive healing. For true healing is neither physical nor mental, but is spiritual in nature. It makes one right with God, allowing, even in sickness or death, a peace and life-quality not often found (Mails, 1991).

I often argue this same point with those who operate solely from the analytical head, rather than including the spiritual heart. True healing begins at the spirit and soul level—beyond the sacred veil. The more we learn to connect with the spiritual realm, the more healing can occur. Each opposite, as previously noted, corresponds to its counter part—the spirit with the mind, the soul with the body. As God heals the soul, we transfer that healing to the body. As He heals the spirit, we transfer that healing to the mind. This does not mean that all illness begins in the spirit and soul, but all cures do.

In the Cherokee practice of healing, the healer learns as much as possible about the patient before attempting to take any therapeutic action. In so doing he is able to find the true source of the pain, which may be psychological or spiritual in nature. It often requires delving deep into the patient's past (a common psychological approach) to find the accurate location of the ailment. Illnesses of the mind, the spirit, or the soul are difficult to trace and often require many sessions in order to appropriately analyze—one reason the modern medical practitioner's system of patient in/patient out, as quickly as possible, does not work.

My good friend and cancer survivor, David Fonde (not merely a survivor, but a valiant warrior of the disease) states that healing begins with a belief in the God-given power of the body to heal itself followed by a commanding visualization of such healing taking place and if necessary, guided imagery, or the loving, yet authoritative, assistance of man or book to assist through the visualization process. In our many discussions we have determined that, though we may "believe" on one level, convincing the mind and body to appropriately respond to our belief, is another matter. We believe, but. And either our spirit, our soul, our mind, or our body picks up on even the minuteness of hesitation, and the transfer of healing does not occur—healing that often has already occurred on a spiritual level.

Spirit-Rituals for the Senses:

"It is neither the quality nor the quantity, but the devotion to sensual savors" (Thoreau, 1965, p. 156). In our journey toward spiritual growth we are encouraged to excommunicate our physical senses, and often rightly so. But, in like manner, through the avenue of ritual, an appropriate devotion to our senses can unlock sheltered channels to that which is spiritual. Calvin Lehew (2003) well states this phenomenon in his book, *Metaphysics 101*. "The American Indians, South American Indians, and African tribes all use visualization in their daily lives. They visualize for rain, good crops, healthy children, healing of the sick. They plant positive thought seeds and then expect positive results. They do dances, light fires or candles, chant incantations, and go through certain rituals. They get kinesthetically, spiritually, and emotionally involved in the whole process ...and get what they ask for" (pp. 104-105). They involve their senses in making spiritual connections. [Calvin Lehew is a friend and fellow journeyman in the spiritual voyage of man. His modern day journalistic ponderings on the subject of the power of visualization are empowering].

It seems our senses can be strictly external impulses of smell, taste, touch, sight, and hearing, or they can include a metaphysical level of instinct generated from the spirit. Rather than a sixth sense, as believed by many, I have come to understand that we are each endowed with a natural, and supernatural, degree of sense. On a day-to-day basis our senses operate on a physical plane, but, if so directed, they will open the pathway to a spiritual plane—the spirit and soul of all things created.

Through our speech (a manner in which we share our breath), our mental thoughts, and our emotions (how we feel), we can also share our spirit. As we listen and hear the words of another, we can share in their spirit. This is the effect of the mind-spirit connection. As we engage in touch, we can share not only our body, but our soul — through the body-soul connection. Through the senses of taste, smell, and vision, we can share our essence — our essence representing the combined elements of spirit and soul. And though it is available to all, few ever experience the senses at this intimate level.

"Listen to the air, You can hear it, feel it, smell it, taste it. Woniya waken — the holy air — which renews all by its breath" (Lame Deer, 1972, p. 108). [Lame Deer was a full-blood Lakota (Sioux) medicine man, born in the late 1800's].

Jung (1957) supports this pattern of thought noting that these internal instincts are anything but blind, for they are in-truth, our inner-man becoming in tune with our external environment — something we might call intuition.

Hearing: "When you're learning something, don't be yakking away. Learn to listen. Listen to the wind. If you're walking along and a covey of birds suddenly flies up in the air, stop. Something disturbed them. What was that something" (Bear Heart, 1998, p. 55).

The spirit-ritual of hearing involves learning to listen with our spirit, not just our mind. And to listen with the spirit requires being able to center and focus the mind, typically through some type of meditative action. We hear all the time, but we seldom listen. In our fast-paced world of overwhelming material structure, we often tear past the gift to get to the box — we miss the inner beauty of that which surrounds us each day to get back to our outward, boring routine.

To better equip yourself to spirit-hear, choose an hour or a day and simply listen to people as they speak. Pay attention to what they are saying, as well as visually observing their non-verbal communication. This is spirit-hearing. We typically are so caught up determining how we will respond that we do not hear what those around us are really saying.

Take a walk in the woods and identify as many sounds as are encountered. Follow each sound to its source, then journal each finding.

Choose an encouraging statement, Bible verse, quote, song, or poem. Read it slowly, openly, and allow it to speak—journal the experience. Don't go to the reading with preconceived ideas about what it will say or what it means.

Take a vow of silence for a day. Notice how much more is experienced when not engaged in speaking.

"For you will go out with joy and be led forth with peace; The mountains and the hills will break forth into shouts of joy before you, and all the trees of the field will clap their hands" (NASB, 1995, Isaiah 55:12). [Isaiah was probably the greatest of the prophets of God. He lived before 700 B.C. His writings were specifically directed at leading the people of Judah back to their Creator].

The sounds made by the creation are not always audible to the human ears, but in-spirit, we will note their sounds. As we in-tune our spirit with that of the Creator and the creation, all that have life will offer forth their song.

Speaking: Our speech has a spiritual connection in that our breath and spirit are intertwined. Throughout history the words spirit, breath, and even wind have been interchangeably expressed. The creation came into being through the breath, or words of the Creator. And still today, we create or tear down with our spoken words, our breath, our spirit.

As previously discussed, we speak much more than we listen, so a spirit-ritual for appropriating our speech must involve speaking with purpose. Create a language of meaning, using words that inspire, encourage, teach, direct, guide, create, and support. Avoid all negative words.

A wonderful exercise is to choose a period of time in which, before we speak, we observe our motives. Hold every word until that word is thought upon. It is also beneficial to write our thoughts down before we share them. Are we trying to impress, have the last word, prove our worth, cause pain or hurt, or simply responding with kindness and love.

When under distress, we can simply repeat a positive phrase in our mind: "All is well with my soul." Or repeat the words "in" and "out" while inhaling and exhaling. Verbally reiterate the fruits of the spirit to encourage their frequent use in your life: love, peace, joy, kindness, patience, goodness, gentleness, faithfulness, and self-control.

The same speaker, and sometimes even the same words, can have a wonderful calming effect, a powerfully inspiring effect, or the intensity to destroy. Through the senses of hearing and speech, we share our spirit. But what kind of spirit are we sharing?

Feeling/Touching: Since the soul is the counterpart to the body and the spirit is the counterpart to the mind, through physical touch we can touch others with our soul, and through words spoken and words thought, we can touch others with our spirit. Likewise, through these physical mediums, we can transmit the Spirit of our Creator which is alive and which works through His creation (us) to touch the world. Through the gift of touch, we feel life and share life.

❖ ❖ ❖

Touch, even sexual touch, should always be sacred touch or spirit-touch. It is the most intimate expression of love we can share with another.

❖ ❖ ❖

Through touch, we receive and release spiritual energy, we speak a language without the need for words, we experience nature's wisdom, and we share our soul with the cosmos. We can learn much about this spirit-ritual of touch by taking the time to experience our sense of touch by feeling and touching that which has life, whether it be a stone, a leaf, an animal, or the human body.

Have someone place objects (some familiar, some unfamiliar) in a closed container. Without looking at the objects, place a hand inside the box and feel and identify each object. If the object is recognized by its feel, it is because it has been experienced before. If never experienced, the object will not likely be identifiable. Why? We must experience touch to comprehend it. If we say we do not like to be touched, it is because we have not been appropriately touched.

Another exercise with nature is to select a tree. Touch the place where the soil joins the trunk, touch the bark and identify the textures, touch a leaf and feel the smoothness or hair-like fibers. Feel the difference in the bark on the trunk and the bark on smaller limbs. If possible, touch the inner-bark and any liquid substance produced by the tree. Feel any life forms which have attached themselves to the tree. And finally, journal your findings with drawings and descriptions.

I have been formally trained in the holistic art of *Healing Touch*, sometimes called touch therapy, or energy touch. In each of these variations the healer touches in a downward and gentle motion. Any negative energy is thus drawn downward, and out of the body. At the same time the body is energized with positive energy generated *through* the healer. Healing Touch typically begins at the head, drawing the energy toward the chin, down the shoulders, neck, arms, hands, chest, back, waist, legs, and feet—although it may also be directly applied to any area of the body in need of healing. Never get in a rush and never draw the energy upward.

In order to better understand the power of healing touch, or to develop as a methodology the ability to spirit-touch, the following activities are recommended—adapted from the *Healing Touch* technique (Healing Touch, Level I Training Notebook, 1996) and from the Cherokee techniques for touch (Mails, 1988).

Warm the hands in a fire, over a warm surface, in warm water, or by rubbing together. The Cherokee would typically warm the hands in a fire. Next, without clothing, or with limited clothing, begin to slowly touch each place on the body (self or another intimate friend), beginning above any place where the body creases or bends. With a gentle, downward stroke of the fingers (fingers slightly apart) start at the upward area and draw the energy to the body's natural fold.

Begin at the center of forehead outward to temples; down the ears to the fold at the base of the ears; begin at the space above the nose though the socket of both closed eyes outward; begin at the center of the mouth outward across the opening of the mouth on both sides; under the chin from the back of the jaw-line downward; across the shoulder blades beginning at the neck outward to the shoulders; down the back on both sides and at the center — downward and out at the base; across the frontal bone running from the shoulders to the base of the neck; under the armpit moving outward; down, around, and under each breast and out at the center; down the inside and outside of the arms from shoulder to elbow; then from elbow to wrist; down the hands; down each finger; down each side of the trunk to the waist; across the waist line outward from the middle to each side; from the inside of the upper thighs following the ridge outward; down the inside and outside of each thigh to the knees and outward; down the lower legs from the knees to the ankles and outward; around each ankle; across the arch of each foot toward the inside of the body; across the base of each foot from heal to toe; and down each toe. Be sure to massage each side of the body and repeat each downward stroke four or seven times — both sacred numbers.

In spirit-touch, the Creator is invited into the ritual of touch, and He is actually the one providing healing energy through the instrument of the warmed healer's hands. Spirit-touch requires the healer to have a clean heart of love. Though this methodology of touch he shares his soul and the Spirit of the Creator. The healer may: simply press the hands over a specific area; gently, and in a relaxed manner, massage a particular region of the body; and apply pressure at any sensitive pressure points which are typically located in the vicinity of, but not directly atop of, an area in pain (usually found by moving the fingers over several inches of skin around the body zone in question).

These areas are located above the eyebrows, at the temples, at the hollow points at the base of the thumb where it joins the wrist, across the shoulders, the muscles in the neck, below the ears, various places on the cheeks, numerous spots on the back (especially near the shoulder blades), and an array of regions on the legs (Mails, 1988).

Experimentation is the best way to find these pressure points. So with your finger tips, gently seek out small, sensitive areas of pain. When you locate these pressure points apply a slow, gentle, counter clockwise motion. In my practice, I have found that this counter clockwise motion seems to more readily loosen areas of tension than a clockwise motion—much like a counter clockwise movement loosens bolts and screws. In fact, I often visualize the action of a wrench loosening a bolt as I manipulate a pressure point.

In spirit-touch the one touching must be totally dedicated to bringing pleasure, stress release, or healing to the one being touched. He or she is not to be thinking about concluding the task in order to receive a massage in return. This spirit of self-seeking will reduce the healing effect of the touch.

Of course touch does not have to always be a full massage, but an understanding of how to provide healing touch or spirit-touch will make any touch more meaningful and will allow the recipient to experience a sensual awakening at the level of the soul. Once understood, this degree of touch can be experienced with something as simple as the holding of hands.

Smelling: What I most remember about my grandparent's farm is the smell of wild spearmint after a spring shower. After my grandfather's passing, my father took and planted some of that spearmint and gave some to me, which I planted by the kitchen door. After a good rain, as I walk by that door, I am instantly transported, in-spirit, back to that old homestead sitting atop a hill in West Tennessee. What a powerful sense that can transport us through space and time, yet we seldom stop to enjoy its sensuous power.

To better learn to appreciate this magnificent sense and to make experiencing smells a priority, there are several exercises in which we can actively participate. Take the time to smell the various foods on the plate before eating them. Smell someone's hair or skin, smell the rain, the earth, the mineral smell in water, a plant, or even the disagreeable odor of a lady bug. Not all smells are pleasant, but all inspire thought. All smells have the capability of transversing the physical boundary of mind and body and reaching the level of the spirit and soul. More than any other sense, except touch, smell is a sacred spirit-sense in that it expresses the essence of its life-form.

We can also be inspired by the sense of smell by placing natural smells in containers around the home or office: tobacco, coffee, vanilla, tea, cinnamon, fruit, sage, natural candles, or flowers. These living smells are often less expensive than artificial scents and much more spirit-inspiring.

Tasting: Within the mouth are hundreds of taste receptors, yet we devour our food so quickly that few are properly activated. With the ritual of spirit-taste, we must slow down and savor the textures, tastes, and smells of our food. A wonderful taste exercise is to take a flavorful food, which is complex in consistency, and allow it to turn and twist in the mouth—under the tongue, against the back of the tongue, touching the roof of the mouth. An item like a cranberry, a flavor infused raisin, or a piece of fruit works well. Chew slowly, with 12 or more bites before swallowing. Consciously acknowledge the various mixture of flavors and attempt to distinguish each one.

The tasting and eating of food can be a simple means of bringing nutrition to our body for survival, or a spiritually sensuous experience. The way of change is through slow, patient, meditative eating. The benefits are extremely holistic in nature, in that we eat less and experience more. We also gain access to the food at the level of its essence — its spirit and soul.

Eating—"He who distinguishes the true savor of his food can never be a glutton; he who does not cannot be otherwise" (Thoreau, 1965, p. 156).

As I was growing up, my family saw sitting down to a meal with each other as a means of sharing, not only food but love and affection. Eating with other people is a ritual in which the participants share in each other's physical existence. We must eat to live, and we seem to draw strength and joy in making others a part of this life experience. If we wish to get to know others, we take them to dinner. And during holidays, we plan special meals with family and friends. Food has become the number one way in which humans commune with each other. Eating should, therefore, become a sacred experience and not simply a hurried process between work and sleep. But how do we make eating a spirit-ritual?

At church, we take communion with God through the sacred elements of bread and wine. We share in His death, burial, and resurrection, but we also share in His life, now and forever. In eating with others we can do the same—we can commune with them on a spiritual level and share in the most intimate aspects of their lives. The key in making this transition, from physical eating to spiritual eating, requires effort—effort in understanding the things held in common and why the people in your life have been placed together with you, in this place, at this given time, in history. There is meaning and purpose in everyone we meet and through the various senses — seeing, hearing, touching, smelling, and tasting—we can find that purpose.

The spirit-ritual of eating begins by identifying the source of our food and the friends with whom it is shared. The source of both goes back to a first-cause. The Creator formed the earth, man, and the life-energy which supports them both—plants, water, sunlight, animals. The farmer plants the crop, the workman harvests, and the hunter hunts. At a building somewhere close by, or far off, someone packages the food into containers. A truck driver delivers the food to a store. A stocker places the food on the shelf, and a clerk places it in a bag. Someone makes the money to buy the food, and someone makes the purchase. The food is brought to the home or restaurant, and a person must prepare it. Then there are those who come to share in the feast.

Life, energy, sweat, and time all go into our ability to eat. It is a very complicated, painstaking task, yet we seldom think beyond the fork in our hand and the food on our plate. Most of us have become so far removed from the process of going out and planting and gathering our own vegetables, from raising and killing our own animals, that food means very little to us today, except for our being ill-tempered when we must wait for it.

We have also grown accustomed to eating by the time-piece on our wrist, rather than the one inside our body. We no longer eat only when we are hungry, we eat all day long. And our bodies show the abuse. Likewise, within the United States, we are overwhelmed by eating establishments which offer the largest portion sizes in the world. No wonder we suffer from obesity and diabetes. The only way to overcome this deadly trend is through the introduction, or reintroduction, of ritualistic eating—through spirit-eating.

Take time before each meal to recognize the source of your bounty. Say a prayer of thanksgiving and pray for the Creator to direct the energy within the food to an appropriate use in your body. Then sit down, eat slowly, savor the flavors and textures, enjoy the friends with whom you are sharing this experience, and stop eating when your body tells you it is full. Eating has now become a spiritual experience.

Fasting—Jewish tradition refers to fasting as "humbling the soul." The soul, being the opposite or counterpart of the body, is more readily available for a connection to be made between soul and body during a fast. Thereby, what benefits the body will also benefit the soul. As we learn about our body—its desires, needs, and drives—we learn about the deepest requests of our soul. For even though we are depriving our body for a short period of time in a fast, our physical senses and pleasures are actually heightened, leading to a union of body and soul.

A typical fast allows the participant to drink water or unsweetened tea, but not food or other calorie infused substances, for a period of 1–3 days. The physical purpose is to de-stress our digestive organs, to flush ourselves of toxins, and allow our body's energies to shift toward more meaningful objectives such as growth and healing. Yet, the holistic benefits of a fast far surpass the mere physical benefits.

A short fast is considered safe for the majority of individuals who are in good health, as long as sufficient liquids are consumed. However, it is not recommended for those who are underweight, pregnant or nursing, or those who have eating disorders, heart problems, diabetes, cancer, or other similar ailments. Any concerns about fasting for more than one day should be discussed with a medical professional.

For a successful spirit-fast: dedicate the time to a mental or spiritual activity like meditation—walking in the woods, journaling, or reading; be realistic in setting goals—typically one day is a good start; pray for success—believe and visualize victory; preplan ways to deal with temptations—someone to call, an activity to participate in, a good movie; cut down on heavy portion sizes, caffeine, and alcohol a few days before the fast; limit physical exertion during the fast; keep water available and drink plenty; upon completion gradually introduce food back—don't gorge the few days after your fast, but slowly introduce foods, paying particular attention to the senses they arouse (Self Healing Newsletter, January 2005).

Seeing: "It is said that 83% of the information the brain receives comes through our eyes and only 11% comes through the ears" (Lehew, 2003, p. 111). What this means is that more people are visual learners than auditory learners. If we don't see it, we don't learn about it. Yet, in getting to know people, places, and things, we spend a tremendous amount of time talking. We are frequently oblivious to the mass array of visual stimulation all around us. Our eyes are often open—they see—yet the connection between our physical brain and eternal spirit goes uncoupled. We can learn much more with our mouths shut and our eyes open than the reverse.

The next time you are with friends or business associates, make a mental note of their personal surroundings. What do they wear, what do they collect, what do they drive, what colors do they like, what is on their walls, is there a diploma telling you of their education, are there family photos, do they have a pet, etc. When you leave, journal your findings. You now have wonderful insight into giving meaningful gifts or creating relevant and meaningful conversation. You are better equipped to provide kindness, love, and service.

"I use my eyes to touch with gentleness and love. You can tell a lot about a person by looking into their eyes, and you can say things to people with your eyes that you cannot say with words. Eyes betray truth or dishonesty" (Mails, 1991, p. 78).

It is difficult to lie when looking directly into another's eyes. These windows into our soul are like mirrors reflecting our individual spirit. With our eyes we share our inward reality. If we have evil in our heart, our eyes will betray us. If we have love in our heart, our eyes display our joy to the world, and others will share in that love.

"Our eyes enable us to touch nature, and to learn from it as we watch the seasons, the different skies, the winds, the grass, the streams and the lakes. We apply these lessons to people and to how we should understand all things" (Mails, 1991, p. 79).

As we spend time out visually absorbing the creation, away from people and man-made things, we learn tremendous life lessons. Why is it that we call a twisted and disfigured tree a thing of beauty, yet a person with the same blemish we call deformed and ugly? Why do we see the cleansing power of the rain, yet strive to still the tears of one who cries? Why do we see that the grass grows best with the appropriate mixture of rain, sunshine, and supporting nutrients, yet we deprive ourselves of the same diversity of nourishment?

Examine these marvelous lessons which are our gifts from nature every single day. Take the time to journal one comparison a day for one week, or take an entire day in nature and journal a number of visual lessons that we as humans can learn from the creation.

We have grossly misunderstood the role for humankind in the whole of nature. For we are only a part of the creation, a fiber in the strand. In fact, the human race was the last of the created elements to be breathed into existence. Yet, we have been granted the awesome responsibility as caretakers of this cosmos which preceded us. What we see with our eyes, we must care for with our heart and in our action. With our mind and body, we must display the desires of the spirit and soul. What we see that needs to be done, we must do. In our seeing and doing, we grow spiritually—no matter how simple the task. For it is often in the most unpretentious of responsibilities that we see beyond the sacred veil.

The Spirit-Ritual of Marriage:

Through the ritual of marriage, a couple can experience the ultimate earthbound relationship—the spiritual union of souls. It is not through the rite of the wedding ceremony that this level of intimacy occurs, rather through the daily recommitment ritual of marriage. If conducted as a spirit-ritual, the ritual of marriage is a ceremony of bliss.

Joseph Campbell (1988) spoke of this ceremony as beginning with the wedding vow: in sickness and health, wealth or poverty. This is a pledge to take the other person as one's center. There the ceremony begins, a pledge to ride together the journeys upward and the journeys downward, yet always holding to the center. The ride, the journey, is following one's bliss. To seek a halt is to abandon the call toward bliss. The ceremony of marriage is intended to be a daily ritual, a daily journey—a never ending spirit-ritual of bliss. Yet, few married couples ever experience marriage at this level of intensity.

"Marriage is not a love affair, it's an ordeal. It is a religious exercise, a sacrament, the grace of participating in another life" (Campbell, Joseph, as selected in Osbon, Diane K., 1991, pp.46-47).

"If you go into marriage with a program, you will find that it won't work. A successful marriage is leading innovative lives together, being open, non-programmed. It's a free fall: how you handle each new thing as it comes along" (Campbell, Joseph, as selected in Osbon, Diane K., 1991, p.47).

"A young husband should remember that a woman sacrifices infinitely more for the man she loves than he does for her, and he should study to prevent early disappointments. If both husband and wife could do this for one another, the divorce courts would be without business" (Marden, 1913, p. 327). [Little could be found about this author, but his philosophy of life can be summed up in his quote as follows: "To be happy, we must

❖ 95 ❖

harmonize with the best thing in us. Real happiness is cheap enough, yet how dearly we pay for its counterfeit"].

"Marriage is a relationship. When you make the sacrifice in marriage, you're sacrificing not to each other but to unity in a relationship. The Chinese image of the Tao, with the dark and light interacting—that's the relationship of yang and yin, male and female, which is what a marriage is…You are no longer this one alone; your identity is in a relationship…It's not simply one's own thing, you see. It is, in a sense, doing one's own thing, but the one isn't just you, it's the two together as one (Campbell, 1988, p.7). This unique form of sacrifice and unity is one in which each partner gives 100%, not 50%. Each person is able to maintain a personal identify while at the same time become one in identity with another person.

But, how do two people retain their separate identities, yet create a new, stronger identity of unity and purpose? How do we learn to sacrifice self for a relationship? How can two physical, human life-forms move from a relationship of flesh and mind to one of religious exercise and experience—a marriage of two spirits and souls growing together?

Well, probably much like you, I have read the books and heard marriage counselors and teachers explain *the right things to do:* communication, listening, romance, respect, honesty, humor, quality time together, and active expressions of love and kindness. And I fully agree that each of these gifts *must* be put into practice until they are learned and shared with our spouses. But, why do we have such a hard time living up to these standards, standards we enter marriage believing we can easily adhere to? Because we enter marriage, "in love."

In *The Road Less Traveled,* Dr. Scott Peck (1978) addressed this "in love" experience, referring to it as an "act of regression" (p.87) and a "collapse of our ego boundaries" (p.89). When we are in love we feel we can do anything, we are invincible. The object of our desire makes us feel marvelously alive and whole. But sooner or later everyone who falls in love, will fall out of love. It is then, and only then, that real love can begin — a love of sacrifice, a spiritual union of souls. This does not mean that romantic feelings of love must stop, but that romance now has its appropriate place and is practiced from the essence of friendship, intimacy, and pure love, rather than as an act of expected reciprocation.

It is unfortunate that most marriages never reach this pinnacle of intimacy. The reason? Because these relationships start on an unsolid foundation, one which never becomes spiritually fortified — they never come to understand and practice the spirit-ritual of marriage.

At an age when we are traditionally most drawn toward marriage (18–28), our mind and body have become significantly separated from our spirit and soul by the powerful attraction of the physical world. If we are blessed with spiritual vision during this time, if we gain glimpses into the sacred realm, we also hear an inward call — the draw of the spirit and soul.

As we listen to the call and make a connection with our Creator, we begin to find individual harmony and union between *our* spirit and soul and the Spirit and Soul of our *Maker*. If we understand the *Principle of Opposites,* we then allow our Creator to work in our lives to bring about harmony on a physical plane as well — our spirit with our mind and our soul with our body.

However, if we are blinded from spiritual vision, our spirit and soul cannot become one with our Maker, and without this metaphysical union, we cannot become one of spirit, soul, mind, and body.

In the spirit-ritual of marriage the same principle applies. If a woman is not at one — her spirit and soul not at one with her mind and body; her spirit, soul, mind, and body not at one with her Creator — and she joins with a man who *is* one, her un-united multiples cannot live in peace and harmony with the man. If neither the man nor the woman is at one, the process toward unity becomes even more insurmountable.

For a perfect union of a man and woman, each must first become one with the Creator and one within, before becoming one with each other is possible. This is why so many marriages fail. The soul-mate principle is real, but it must begin with a metaphysical awakening; it cannot be supported upon the bases of physical attraction alone. The spirit-ritual of marriage requires individual unity, individual oneness, before two different individuals can ever become one. It is only when our spirit and soul hear the call of God and our mind and body follow suit that we can find our true soul-mate. Spend time actively participating in the spirit-rituals within this chapter and open your mind and body to be touched from beyond the sacred veil. Become one with your Maker and one with yourself. Then, and only then, will you be equipped to become one with another person.

The Spirit-Ritual of Romance:

Romance should never go away in a marriage relationship, but unless it evolves into spirit-romance, it most certainly will. The emotions of romance typically grow out of three different scenarios: attraction which turns to romance; friendship which becomes attraction, followed by romance; and friendship which turns to intimate friendship, followed by attraction and romance. Each of these initial degrees of romance are proceeded by, and based upon, physical attraction. At this elemental level, romance becomes a part of a relationship for entirely selfish motives — we give romance in order to receive romance in return. We become romantically involved for what it does for self, not for the person to whom we are showing romance. If romance remains at this level, it will slowly fade away or even abruptly vanish.

How then do we make romance more spiritually meaningful — how do we keep romance alive and well? Through the spirit-ritual of romance. Spirit-romance is based on friendship, intimacy, or oneness, not merely physical attraction. It is emotion and action for a higher purpose. In spirit-romance the giver receives joy in the giving. It is not rooted in expectation of return. In the spirit-ritual of romance there must be sacrifice. The giver spends time and thought in the choice of gifts; in the planning of a date or trip; or in the words penned in a letter, poem, or song. It has nothing to do with what the giver wants, but is all about providing pleasure for the recipient. Spirit-romance, then, begins with an examination of our individual motives, followed by an examination of what the recipient would most enjoy.

To take part in the spirit-ritual of romance we must learn all we can by studying our partner or potential partner. What colors do they like, what collectables do they appreciate, what type of music do they listen to, what books do they read, what styles of clothing do they wear, what subjects do they discuss, do they like the sunshine or the snow, what are their favorite foods, do they like specific types of animals; etc. All of these peculiarities are expressions of the individual spirit and will assist in the connection of mind and spirit in both the giver and the receiver.

Once the interpersonal research has been mentally complied, we can utilize the information to appropriately romance the person of our desires. But remember, we must find joy in the planning, in the searching for the right gift, or the smile on their face, not on the expectation that they will do something in return. And also keep in mind that this type of romance does not have to be financially burdensome; it just has to come from one heart which has learned how to connect with another.

The Name Giving Spirit-Ritual:

In many of the mystical prayer formulas of the Cherokee, the shaman would speak the name and the clan of the individual when asking for healing, love, or destruction. It was believed that the speaking of one's name evoked power, and by the appropriate use of the name, fitting results would follow. Still today, to the Indian, a name is not simply a label by which someone is called, but it is an extension of the personality, just as much so as an arm or leg. Therefore, this name, just like any bodily appendage, can become damaged and in need of repair. For this reason a shaman might go to water, or through other suitable ceremonies to identify a patient with a new name, allowing the client a fresh start in life (Mooney, 1891).

For most of us, changing our name is not an option we will likely undertake. Yet, it is extremely important for each of us to find meaning, purpose, and power in our name. We start by asking our parents questions about our name: how it was selected, what it means, what it means to them, etc. If named after someone, we should find out all we can about that person—his/her personality and characteristics, what he/she did for a living, when he/she lived. If the research reveals positive meaning, then we should hold a ceremony in which we take the name we were given and accept it, along with its individual meaning and purpose.

If, however, the research reveals negative findings concerning the background of our name, the name doesn't have to change, just the meaning. For in truth, all names hold both positive and negative meaning depending on the individuals who carried that name before us. We must simply find a meaning that applies to who we are and who we wish or need to become. We can again hold a ceremony, but this time we ask friends and family to share what we mean to them and the characteristics they like about our personality. If our name is truly an extension of our personality, then we, individually, give meaning and purpose to our name. Once our friends have shared what that meaning is, then we ceremonially take our name and formally accept it. Through the process of either one of these spirit-rituals, we infuse energy, power, and meaning into our name and, thereby, into our whole person.

The Spirit-Ritual of Exercise:

Why do we eat three times a day? Why do we go to bed about the same time every evening? Why do we travel the same roads to our office every day? It is not because we need to eat three times a day, or that we must be in bed by ten o'clock, or that there are no other ways to get to work. Rather, it is because we have developed a ritual, and come what may, we are going to follow our routine.

This simple fact of life, though often self-limiting, is the only way I have found for human beings to adhere to an exercise program—it must become a ritual. And as a physical ritualistic activity alone, it will most certainly benefit our physical being. But as a spirit-ritual, it will benefit not only our body, but our spirit and mind, soul and body.

The spirit-ritual of exercise begins by finding an exercise that activates and motivates the inward man. It must have spirit-content. Remember, all things created have spirit, or spiritual essence. Therefore, a spirit-ritual, be it eating or exercising, must relate to the creation in some manner: walks in nature, listening to nature sounds during an exercise routine, exercising with a good friend, paying attention to breathing during exercise (there is a strong connection between the breath and spirit), meditation, etc. Yet, most formal exercise programs are designed to take place within the sterile confines of an indoor facility, void of spirit other than the people taking part in the exercises.

The new Western acceptance of Eastern exercise programs such as Tai Chi, Yoga, Breathworks, and Meditation are wonderful examples of spirit-ritual exercises. They each assist the participant in connecting with the spirit. Earlier we discussed the evidence that spirit-ritual is the pathway to the sacred. So, in spirit-exercises we look for activities which encourage the union of our mind with our spirit. It is important that we choose exercises which are enjoyable; ones in which we can willingly, consistently, and routinely take part; ones which involve elements of the creation; and ones in which we can pay attention to our breathing. The goal is for the program to become as ritualistic as our eating and sleeping habits.

The Give-Away Spirit-Ritual:

The Cherokee have long believed that material possessions disturb the physio-spiritual balance of man. Public giving, known as give-away ceremonies, are therefore often held as a way to purify the participant and to honor someone in need.

Medicine Bags: To the Native American, the word "medicine" means "the power to change." Items placed within a medicine bag are typically items that assist the holder with this transformation and are gifts from those who hold meaning in their lives.

The spirit-ritual of the medicine bag ceremony has become a vital part of the Smokey Mountain Spirituality Class I teach each year. During this one week retreat each student creates a small medicine bag which is then worn around the neck, beneath the shirt. As the students learn about each other and share in emotional, spiritual, and physical experiences, they collect small items that represent each new relationship.

On the final day a medicine bag ceremony is held and a give-away takes place in which each student shares a special gift with each classmate. This ceremony has become an extremely intimate and sacred activity which teaches students to share their spirit with another through experience, then to share their spirit through a metaphorical gift which represents the experience.

A medicine bag and its contents are traditionally a very private matter, and the contents are only known to the holder of the medicine bag and the one who has given something to be placed within the bag. In this group activity the group has become one with each other individually, thus allowing the group as a whole to become one. Therefore the contents are known to all and are kept as a reminder of the strength and power gained through the sharing of a spiritual journey. Each item within the medicine bag now holds special psychological and spiritual influence to guide the recipient toward change—Medicine.

Medicine bags can also be created solely by the individual, with special sacred items selected and placed within the bag which represent spiritual strength, power to change, spiritual growth and development, or sacred relationships. The keeper of the bag will ask the Creator to infuse each item with the power to assist the keeper in making appropriate choices, and appropriate changes, in life in order to remain spiritually strong and whole.

The Spirit-Ritual of Detachment:

"Our attachments are unnecessary psychological and spiritual baggage" (Walsh, 1999, p. 51). They are things that we allow to control our ability to find true joy because we are so caught up in the coarser aspects of life. "What is more common than to see men and women starve the soul, and paralyze the growth and expansion of the finer sentiments, which alone make life worth living, for the sake of the coarser pleasures of the senses, or in order to pile up material wealth, the effect of which is, as a rule, to draw us farther and farther away from the life of the spirit" (Marden, 1913, pp. 73-74)?

The answer? In the words of Thoreau (1965), "Simplicity, simplicity, simplicity" (p. 71). All of us desire happiness and joy. Do we not? Yet we continue to seek happiness in the collection of *things*. These things may be possessions such as cars, houses, money, or even relationships, but sooner or later these possessions seem to end up possessing us. Our seeking after happiness may also lead us to search for that which is sensual: power, prestige, popularity, beauty, or sex. Yet these gifts, once granted, quickly loose their appeal.

One thing that has consistently been handed down, not only by existentialists like Thoreau, but by all the major spiritual movements and religions, is that physical possessions and worldly ambitions, along with their endless attractions, will not bring about long-lasting happiness. Yet, for the thousands of years that this has been a proven reality, we have continued to be caught in a trance by the allure of things. Chuang Tzu, known as one of the greatest Taoist Sages (one who has transcended beyond the physical) describes our predicament well: "You use all your vital energy on external things and wear out your spirit" (Walsh, 1999, p. 32).

This line of thinking, then, brings up the question: do worldly possessions bring us *any* happiness? Scientific research says yes, but only to the point at which our basic needs are met; after that, even though we often seek more and more, the extra *stuff* brings very little additional satisfaction.

It is not that these physical things are inherently bad. In fact, many are good, especially those that are gifts from God and His creation. But the problem arises when we become attached to these worldly belongings—when we think we must have them in order to be happy, fulfilled, complete, or to experience peace or joy. Again, all the great spiritual movements say we must let go of our attachments, or we will greatly suffer. "Most of the luxuries, and many of the so-called comforts of life, are not only not indispensable, but positive hindrances to the elevation of mankind" (Thoreau, 1965, p. 18). Our attachments to excess can never be fully satisfied. They, therefore, keep us tied to the elementary pleasures of life and deprive us from the greatest pleasures.

It is okay to desire good things—peace, a wonderful spouse, less stress, or a good job—but when we "must have these things" in order to enjoy life, we will most definitely suffer. To desire good things is to simply want something and to positively seek after it. On the other hand, to be attached to something is a compulsive disorder. If we desire something and this desire is not fulfilled, we can usually go forward without great languish. But, when an attachment is not fulfilled, we are typically angry, stressed, and in great physical and emotional pain.

Budda's *Four Noble Truths* summarize this reality: *Life is full of difficulties and suffering; the cause of this suffering is our cravings and attachments; letting go of our cravings and attachments will bring freedom from our suffering; freedom from attachment and suffering is only available from living a spiritual life of ritualistic insight, emotion, and action, though which one is transformed* (Kulananda, 2001). [Kulananda is an ordained member of the Western Buddhist Order, whose work is to help Westerners understand and practice Buddhism].

The detachment rituals associated with the entire process of fulfilling these Noble Truths may become harder the further we go into the practice, because we typically save our most constrictive shackles for last. And often, though we might eventually learn to *let go* of certain attachments, we have an extraordinarily difficult time in *relinquishing* what we have let go. Perhaps when we do something for others we still wish to keep the control. We give a gift, but wish to tell the recipient how to use it. We give money and demand the way it is to be spent. To truly detach, we must give, let go, and renounce. Only by mentally disavowing any remaining ownership can we become free from our attachments.

So what is the message for those of us who still have attachments? We must accept the fact that we all have attachments, that we hold much too tightly to our attachments, and we suffer greatly because of our stubborn control.

And why do we hang on to this control? For some things, we do not yet realize our attachment. In addition, we are so caught up in what the world deems important, that we have lost our connection with the spiritual. We are so far removed from our spiritual self, our inner-spirit, and our relationship to our Creator that we feel weak and inferior, so we search for anything that will hide our deficiencies. Yet, we are searching in the world for what we can only find within. We honestly believe in our mind that once we get these earthly trinkets we will finally be happy, content, free from worry and stress. Once we get that perfect job, friends who act the way we want them to, more money, or a peaceful environment, that all will then be most wonderful.

Two eternal problems with this way of thinking are:

1. Some things can never be—a stress free life, a constant peaceful environment, people who always act the way we desire, a perfect job, etc.

2. Those things which can be ours will only bring short-term gratification. "We can never get enough of what we don't really want" (Walsh, 1999, p. 40). (I might replace the word *want* with *need*.)

So what then is the answer to the control our attachments constantly hold over our lives? According to Walsh (1999), we must first change our mind about what we think we need—do we really need that extra food, that inappropriate sexual experience, the overtime at work, a new house, a negative relationship, etc? Once we truly realize that joy and true happiness are not to be found in feeding our attachments, but in relinquishing them, we have knowledge of the path we must follow. But how do we follow this path? For knowledge alone does not empower us.

Unhappiness, stress, and worry are the difference between what we've got to have and what we actually have. If we let go of our attachments by accepting that which we have, this gap dissolves, and along with it our discontent (Walsh, 1999). The only way we can accept what we have as enough, is to realize that what we have is a gift from God and is sufficient for all good works toward which we are called.

We must also relinquish our attachments into the hands of the Creator, asking Him to keep their control far from us. We acknowledge and perhaps even honor their power, yet turn them over to a Greater Power. And we do this through the spirit-ritual of detachment. Within our physical limitations, we *cannot* relinquish this control. Only with the spiritual power of our inner-spirit, energized by its Creator, can we accomplished this mission.

Stress Tree: The next time a mental anxiety is encountered (stress, anger, jealousy, guilt, etc.), trace it back, like you would a family tree, to its source and determine your attachment. The emotions of mental anxiety are painful, and pain is a signal that something is wrong. We must not just treat the symptom of pain, but must get at the root of the problem. Your attachment may even be to something that is positive, like a desire for peace. But to require external peace in order to have internal peace is an attachment and will cause unnecessary suffering. To desire this peace, and to even work toward this peace, is admirable, but to require it brings misery.

Experience a Craving (Walsh, 1999): As a craving enters the mind, closely examine the feelings and emotions experienced. Is there anger, physical pain, or tension? Examine each experience, recognizing its painful effects. We are often so caught up in a craving that we do not take the time to realize the bad things it is doing to us, which are usually much more negative than any possible positive benefits we can derive from fulfilling the craving.

Frustrate a Craving (Walsh, 1999): Choose something desired, and the next time there is a strong craving, deliberately go without it for one hour, half a day, or a day—sex, food, television, speaking angry words, etc. Start with a goal you know you can accomplish, because you need to see that you can be successful. Psychologically and physiologically, many cravings lessen within the hour. Addictive cravings sometimes require days or sometimes a lifetime.

Detachment Box: The Cherokee have a detachment prayer formula where they cover over an enemy, or problem, by blocking them/it from view. This practice has been expanded to the concept of a small detachment box, where in you place a piece of paper upon which you have written the names of individuals or items from which you need to detach yourself—people or items of which you need to let go. Place the box in a place empty of anything else. Cover the box entirely with a black cloth, blocking it from view. As you drape the cloth, repeat four to seven times a prayer emphasizing that the item of concern is being let go into the hands of God, and that it will diminish in your mind by the power of the Creator over your spirit. Something similar to "I cover you over and by the power of God remove your control." For the next four to seven days, contemplate letting go of the person or item through prayer, reinforcing the detachment process. After the chosen time period, remove the cloth and dispose of the box. Leave the black cloth lying flat for four or seven more days as a reminder of your letting go (Mails, 1988, p. 247).

Burden Bag—River Stones: The burden bag of river stones is another ceremonial activity participated in by my Smokey Mountain Spirituality Class. The students each create a list of specific items needed to achieve spiritual wellness—a better relationship to a particular individual, more patience, the ability to more readily forgive, etc. I have found it useful to go out into nature, find a bridge which crosses a river or creek lined with river stone, have the students sketch the bridge, noting the items they listed as needs, available on the other side of the bridge. Then I ask them to list those things that are getting in the way of crossing the bridge.

Now each participant gathers river stones of the appropriate size to represent each burden which is hindering spiritual growth, and the stones are placed in a burden bag (a cloth bag, backpack, or pouch pre-selected for this activity). The keepers of the bags now carry the weight of the burden bag around all day, or multiple days. The burden bag of stones is a metaphorical representation of the mental and spiritual baggage we each carry around on a regular basis—our unwillingness to let go of our burdens. Over a period of hours or days, each participant contemplates each burden, one at a time, while holding the representative stone in his hands. And when ready, each burden is released, symbolically, as the stone is buried, tossed off a cliff, thrown into the river, or disposed of as felt appropriate.

It is important to discuss that the keeper of each bag does not have to be at the point where he knows, without question, that he can let go of each burden before releasing each stone. But the releasing of a stone is meant to initiate a commitment, and serve as a reminder to not only release each burden, but to relinquish it as well — to no longer allow the burden to hinder life experiences and spiritual growth. The releasing of each stone also signifies the acceptance of power granted by our Maker to release and relinquish.

Fire Tags: Upon a piece of paper, or one of the stringed tags often used to price antique furniture, write out your feelings of frustration, your anger, your burdens — this can even be toward someone who has passed away. Hold the paper in your hands, pray and contemplate what you have written, and ask God to infuse you with the power to forgive, release, and relinquish into His hands your burden. Slowly place the paper, or fire tag, into a flame and watch it create smoke which symbolically lifts your prayers before the Creator. As the ashes from the smoke begin to fall, realize that your prayers have been answered, and you indeed have been granted the power to overcome. "So I tell you to ask for things in prayer. And if you believe that you have received those things, then they will be yours" (Holy Bible, Easy to Read Version, 2000, Mark 11:24).

The spirit-ritual of detachment can work with any item of which you wish to let go. The key is to ritualistically connect with the One Who Made You and release your burden into His hands. For He is the only One who has the ability to release you from the control of your attachments. Most any spirit-ritual will assist with the connection; these ritualistic activities are simply meant to help with the aspect of releasing and relinquishing.

The Spirit-Ritual of Going to Water:

In the beginning, before there was time as we know it, there was the Master of All That Has Life, the One We Call God, the Creator. The earth and sky were the first of His creations, but the earth was a wasteland of emptiness. Nothing lived upon the water or the wasteland, and darkness covered the face of the deep void. But God's Spirit hovered over the water like an eagle hovers over its nest of young, for within these watery depths was pre-birth. From the contents of this eternal flow and the wasteland of emptiness, God would impregnate the universe.

Since the beginning of time, water has been in existence. It was either created by God as He fashioned the sky and earth, or it pre-existed each. Either way, water is the oldest, or one of the oldest, elements of the created cosmos (water, sky, and earth). And therein lies the motivation for its historic and universal employment in many forms of ritual. "A field of water betrays the spirit that is in the air. It is continually receiving new life and motion from above" (Thoreau, 1965, p. 137).

Water first came up from the earth, then fell from the heavens in its ever cycling evolution of motion. It flows into man and out as well—over seventy percent of human weight consists of water based fluids. Without sufficient water, man will die; without sufficient water, all of creation will die, for water is a life force that indwells all that was made.

Physical man is born of the water—the watery home of a child within the womb. Spiritual man is said to be born of water and of the Spirit of God in re-birth. The traditional Christian faith holds that a man is first born into a relationship with the *world* through the water of the womb and at this time receives his spirit. The sacred waters of baptism, then, enter man into a relationship with *God*, were-in the Spirit of the Creator comes to live within the newly cleansed spirit of man in re-birth (John 3:5, Acts 2:38). Baptism is symbolic cleansing—"not the removal of dirt from the flesh, but an appeal to God for a good conscience" (NASB, 1995, 1 Peter 3:21).

Whereas the dust of the ground is used for true burial, water can serve as a symbolic burial—water acting as a metaphor for soil, burial as a metaphor for death. "Or do you not know that all of us who have been baptized into Christ Jesus have been baptized into His death? Therefore we have been buried with Him through baptism into death, so that as Christ was raised from the dead through the glory of the Father, so we too might walk in newness of life" (NASB, 1995, Romans 6:3–4).

I find it interesting that evil spirits do not seem to like water—the very element through which God chooses to enter the human body and soul. In Luke 11:24 it states that when an evil spirit exits a man, it travels through *waterless* places to find rest. The evil spirits sent out of the man in Mark 5:13 and Luke 8:33 asked to be placed into another living being—swine. This wish was granted them by the Christ, and I used to wonder why He did not simply destroy the evil. But the rest of the story follows. The pigs ran madly off a cliff and were drowned—The evil spirits were sent to water, in which they could not exist. Water has the power not only to cleanse us of dirt, but from evil as well.

Throughout history we have utilized water's ritualistic power to cleanse and restore our sense of well-being. Most every culture has a flood story in its past. This flood was a cleansing of the earth from all who no longer recognized and followed their Creator. Only a few, "That is, eight persons were brought safely through the water" (NASB, 1995, 1 Peter 3:20).

Since that cleansing flood, we have: rested beside still waters, meditated to the sound of a gentle stream or fountain, savored the rich flavor of mineral waters from deep within the earth, soaked in bubbling hot springs to rejuvenate our body and mind, reclined in the steam of a sweat lodge to purify our soul, bathed under the intensity of a forceful shower, dipped our hands in holy water, and been baptized in the sacred waters of holy forgiveness. It seems that man is drawn to water for life and afterlife.

The Cherokee concept of going to water is a pre- and post-ceremonial cleansing activity in which the participant goes to running water and immerses several times — tradition often notes dipping 7 times. The ritual is said to hold the power of renewal and purification, as well as being utilized as a preparatory rite preceding an ultimate ritual, and a cleansing rite following an activity or action (Mooney, 1891). Many other tribes and cultures also utilize immersion as a preparatory ceremony, as well as cupping water in the hands and allowing it to pour over the arms or body as a metaphorical cleansing sacrament.

Both Mooney (1891) and Adair (1775) document this sacred ceremony among the Cherokee. "In the coldest weather, and when the ground is covered with snow, against their bodily ease and pleasure, men and children turn out of their warm houses or stoves, reeking with sweat, singing their usual sacred notes, *Yo Yo*, and at the dawn of day, adoring *YO He WaH*, at the gladsome sight of the morn; and thus they skip along, echoing praises, till they get to the river, when they instantaneously plunge into it. After bathing, they return home, rejoicing as they run for having so well performed their religious duty, and thus purged away the impurities of the preceding day by ablution (Adair, 1775, p. 127). [James Adair was a descendant of the Fitzgeralds of Ireland. He lived among many Native tribes during his lifetime (with the Cherokee in the early 1700's). Much of his research concludes that the Cherokee are direct descendents of the Hebrew, from the lost Jewish tribes of Israel].

Mails (1996) insists that the traditional Cherokee act of going to water was practiced as a religious responsibility rather than for physical cleansing. The participant would arise before daylight, sing a sacred song, meditate, then precede to a creek and plunge beneath its waters. The most devoted participated each day as a method of purifying any defilement from the previous day or night. This action prepared them as "fit tubes or channels through which God is willing to enlighten people and perform his miracles" (pp. 132-133).

Mails (1988) found that running water is believed to hold powers that a stagnant pool of water does not. A power instilled in the water by the Creator. The early Jewish and Christian faiths held similar views, in that there are Biblical notations of water sources, when stirred by the heavens, holding healing and curative powers. Water for ritualistic purposes should, therefore, be taken from a source of running water.

Each of these rituals of going to water, whether dipping seven times in a creek, pouring water over the arms and body, taking part in a sweat lodge ceremony, or "putting on Christ" in the spirit-ritual of baptism, are cleansing rites which set aside the past and prepare the participant for something yet to come. They each unlock the participant's spirit, so that he may be used as a channel, or vessel, through which communication from God may take place.

But, is the cleansing power in the water, in the personal action of the one going to water, from the Creator of the water, or from all three? I would say all three, in that the spiritual power of the Creator still stirs people, and sacred elements, to serve His purpose, but the people must have a willing heart and allow themselves to be touched by the Spirit of God. The spirit-ritual of going to water is one way in which we can actively open that door of communication. We must cleanse our hearts in order to receive spiritual wisdom and power. We must cleanse our hearts in order to receive saving grace. We must cleanse our hearts in order to "get into" a relationship with God.

The Spirit-Ritual of Meditation:

"Every one should be able to dominate his own mentality, to be the master of his own mind at all times. It is pitiable to see a strong man in most things, a passive victim to the torturing thoughts which he should be able to strangle in an instant" (Marden, 1913, p. 261).

During our day to day functioning, our mind and body should operate under the guidance of our parasympathetic nervous system — which keeps us at an even, calm pace. During times of high stress, our sympathetic nervous system is meant to shift into place, allowing us to meet immediate demands placed upon our mind and body. When this transfer happens, adrenalin and cortisol flood the blood stream, speeding up the heart rate, raising the blood pressure, tensing the muscles, and changing our breathing from deep within our lungs to rapid and shallow breaths from the upper chest.

The problem we face in today's fast-paced world is that the average person remains in a state of constant stress, seldom allowing the body to revert back to the parasympathetic system, which would readily permit our mind and body to relax.

The purpose for meditation is to slow the mind, thus allowing both the mind and body to relax. The purpose for the spirit-ritual of meditation is to make a connection between the mind and spirit, so that the spirit gains control of the mind, thus allowing the parasympathetic nervous system to maintain control. When this happens, chemicals are released which reduce the heart rate, lower blood pressure, relax the muscles, and appropriately regulate breathing.

Until we learn this process of spirit-meditation, we will continue to "live lives of aimless distraction" (Warren, 2002, p. 32). All we have to do is attempt to concentrate on anything for even a brief moment, and we quickly find that our mind has its own mind. Buddhism refers to this aimless mind as the *wild and crazy monkey mind*, erratically leaping from limb to limb — or thought to thought. Our out of control mind keeps us awake, makes us sick, and encourages us to say and do things that we typically would not say and do. Yet day in and day out, we continue to allow it to wreak its havoc.

However, if we learn the art of controlling our mind, we, likewise, learn to control our physical and spiritual well-being as well. We gain the ability to give up addictions, alter our negative emotions, and even control our outward behavior—all by learning to control our mind. If our mind remains out of control, our body and spirit will follow suit. For in our body, we are slaves to our mental restlessness and are helpless to its erratic whims. How then do we begin the process of spirit-meditation?

Our spirit lives within our body, but on a higher plane which also extends outside our body—our aura. It is hard for man to grasp this concept, because it is not inside like our kidneys or lungs, but inside on a higher plane. Sometimes by thinking deep within our mind we can connect with our spirit; other times it helps to think outside our body in order to get a feel for this higher plane. Either way, the mind must first be altered in order to make a spiritual connection between the mind and spirit. This process of mind-slowing begins with breath-work.

Breath-Work: By mimicking the parasympathetic nervous system—by taking full, slow breaths from deep within the lungs—we can begin to bring the mind and the body back into a more relaxed state of being. Cherokee medicine men have long recognized the importance of proper breathing as the essential element necessary in achieving a meditative state of being. A common Cherokee practice is to visualize the inhaled breath interning the body through the outstretched and spread fingers, up through the arms, into the chest, and down into the abdomen; and on the exhale, pressed down through the groin, the legs, and out the feet (Mails, 1988, p. 236).

Another common breath-work ritual is to choose an activity, or a time of day, during which a focus will be placed on deep-breathing—while sitting at a red light, each time the phone rings, before speaking, upon rising from bed in the morning, etc. Each and every time this situation presents itself take four deep breaths. Concentrate on each inhale as an influx of positive spiritual energy *(chi)*, upon each exhale as the release of negative energy. If the mind wanders from this effort, slowly and gently draw it back. Breathe in to the count of the sacred number seven. Hold the breath for a count of four. Then exhale to the count of seven plus four—eleven.

During the inhalation and exhalation of breath-work, one might also concentrate on positive thoughts or words such as repeating various names for God: Creator, Father, Spirit, Jesus, Lord, Holy One, Anointed One, etc. Or, concentrate on the Fruits of the Spirit of God: Love, Peace, Joy, Kindness, Patience, Faithfulness, Gentleness, Goodness, and Self-Control.

Other Meditation Preparation: Often our approach to meditation is an attempt to immediately transfer from an active state of mind and body to a relaxed state, without providing the process for this transfer to adequately take place. In addition to breath-work, there are a variety of tools one might utilize to prepare the mind to meditate.

One might listen to meditative music, take a sweat bath, or take a walk in nature—away from man-made obstacles. If in a natural environment, a focus might be placed on a cloud, a tree, an animal, a plant, a mountain, or a stream. Or even without this focus, the action of walking, or any other physical act, can help slow the mind. If at home or work, a focus can be placed on various parts of the body—beginning with the head and moving downward to the feet, tensing and releasing muscles at each section.

Bear Heart's key to entering a meditative state was to shut his eyes and roll them upward toward the forehead. As noted before, whenever the mind is drawn away from the attempted focus, slowly and gently draw the attention back—repeat this as often as necessary.

Sacred Pondering: Thoreau believed that the early morning was the best time for meditation: "All memorable events, I should say, transpire in morning time and in a morning atmosphere (Thoreau, 1965, p. 68).

Find a good book (The Bible, Emerson, Thoreau, Oswalt Chambers). Read only a short section at a time. Then, just be still and let thoughts come to you about the topic of your reading. Let meaning, or various analogies, present themselves, and then allow for time to spiritually decipher the messages.

The practice of ritualistic pondering, within itself, causes us to slow down, placing our mind in a more meditative state of consciousness or unconsciousness. The spirit-ritual of pondering slows the clutter of the mind, creating a pleasurable patience in which the spirit can be heard.

Luring/Visioning: The Cherokee, the Lakota, and many other Native American tribes have long used the meditative practice of luring, or visioning, to bring what they desired before them. The Cherokee still create luring masks which are worn over the face. These masks are designed to look like and represent the desire, often an animal such as a bear or deer. They may also represent desires such as peace, joy, or patience. The power of these masks begins in the visioning of what is desired. Modern science calls this process imaging or visualization — placing before the mind the process and end result of a desire. This method is often used today, by the medical profession, in the treatment of diseases such as cancer — visualization of the cancer cells being attacked and killed by the healing processes of the body. And the process has proven to be quite effective.

Fools Crow called this procedure luring. This great Lakota holy man emphasized an importance in the ritualistic aspect of the practice as commencing with a visioning of what is desired within the mind, whether it be a person or an attribute. The visioning process was then followed by the creation of a physical representation of the desire. This depiction can be drawn on a piece of paper, traced on the ground with a stick, formed out of wood, or any other method available. Fools Crow would then sit down facing his created symbol, close his eyes, and center himself by taking seven deep breaths. During centering, he would often cup his open hands, signifying his readiness to be filled with spiritual energy.

Next he opened his eyes, focused on the metaphorical picture he had created, and sang a sacred song, or prayer, four times. As he looked off into the distance he would see the person or item awaiting him. After watching for several minutes, he would again close his eyes, look upward toward his forehead, and a white cloud would be formed. This cloud began to move outward toward the object of desire, enclosed the desire, and brought it back to Fools Crow. He believed that at this point, the desire had been fulfilled mentally and spiritually, and that it would soon come to pass on a physical plane as well.

When asked if evil or selfish desires could be lured, Fools Crow stated that most anything could be lured either by means of physical or spiritual power, but that the selfish use of spiritual power, or the acquisition of evil powers, would always come back and attack the lurer (Mails, 1991). When done for spiritually positive desires, and followed with affirmative action, luring or visioning is a very effective ritual for making one's desires come true.

Spirit-Rituals in Nature and the Creation:

"If you would learn the secrets of Nature, you must practice more humanity than others" (Thoreau, 2000, p. 33).

"A respect for creation emerges out of our perceived need for maintaining balance in the world around us. Thus, Indian spirituality is characteristically oriented towards balancing of the world, and our participation in it, both in every-day personal and family actions, and the periodic ceremonies of clans, societies, and whole communities" (Kidwell, Noley, & Tinker, 2001, p. 41).

"The Lakota was a true naturist—A lover of nature. He loved the earth and all things of the earth, the attachment growing with age. The old people came literally to love the soil, and they sat or reclined on the ground with a feeling of being close to a mothering power. It was good for the skin to touch the earth and the old people liked to remove their moccasins and walk with bare feet on the sacred earth" (Chief Standing Bear, as quoted in Mcluhan, 1971, p. 6). [Chief Standing Bear of the Lakota spent his early years of the 1800's on the plains of South Dakota and Nebraska].

For "The Great Spirit is our Father, But the earth is our mother. She nourishes us; that which we put into the ground she returns to us and healing plants she gives us likewise. If we are wounded, we go to our mother and seek to lay the wounded part against her, to be healed. Animals too, do thus, they lay their wounds to the earth" (Bedagi, as quoted in Mcluhan, 1971, p. 22). [Bedagi was an Indian of the Webanakis Nation, a tribe who lived on the Kennebec River but are now long gone].

Our "kinship with the earth is partly love and concern for the earth, but it goes deeper than that. As we abide in Christ, there comes to many of us a sense of being part of the earth. We feel within us the moving of power, so that we can speak forth the word and know that through that word an actual energy is entering into the earth, or the wind, or the clouds, or water, so that it will obey God through us" (Sanford, A., 1983, p. 160).

And as sacred elements of the creation, that which has been created can also teach us, bring power and wisdom to us, and present before us the presence of God. For though "A tree cannot talk, the Creator can communicate to us through any means—a bird, and animal, even a blade of grass" (Bear Heart, 1998, p. 54).

Likewise, these entities are placed here on earth, by the Creator, to serve and to heal us. "Every blade of grass, every leaf, even one pine needle, is trying to filter out some of the pollution that we cause" (Bear Heart,

1998, p. 175). Yet, "We've been very poor stewards of all that was given to us in its pure form. Instead we have become exploiters and abusers of the very thing that sustains our lives, and we think we have nothing to learn from the world around us" (Bear Heart, 1998, p. 169).

But, if we will simply spend time as spiritual students of nature, we will begin to develop an aesthetic super-consciousness that transcends visual stimulation—the artistic and sacred aspects of nature will be brought into our conscious awareness. Therefore, I believe that one who does not believe in God, one who is not spiritually minded, is one who has not spent quality time with nature. For the world of nature shouts to us about God (Romans, Psalms).

Conclusion—if we are to truly grow spiritually, we must spend more quality time taking part in spirit-rituals out in nature and the creation.

❖ ❖ ❖

The Vision Quest: "How long we may have gazed on a particular scenery and think that we have seen and known it, when at length, some bird or quadruped comes and takes possession of it before our eyes, and imparts to it a wholly new character" (Thoreau, 2000, p.36).

"If we really want to know ourselves, at some point in life we're going to have to surrender to a Higher Wisdom who knows all about us—our weakness, our mistakes, and our potentials. Many Native American tribes do that through our meditation known as a vision quest—the setting aside of a time and place, alone out in nature, to communicate with a Higher Being and explore that which is within" (Bear Heart, 1998, p. 230).

It seems to me, the gaze of mankind is habitually misdirected, for we continue our unfruitful search for meaning and answers below the spiritual horizon. Thoreau (1965) expresses it well: "The mass of men lead lives of quiet desperation" (p.14). I believe this desperation stems from our letting the consistent, yet irregular, complexities of our day-to-day environment keep us from entering a state of meditation or a surrendering of our spirit and mind to God. In the chaos of daily life it is profoundly difficult to enter a state of meditation. The vision quest, out in nature, is one methodology which aids in this endeavor of an inward and upward orientation.

Man, in his industrialized withdrawal from nature, has ceased to be astonished by the phenomenon presented everyday within the creation. Re-exposure to these life-supporting elements can activate and energize the spirit. For in the collective bonds of all things created, there is something which draws our spirit mightily upward. As our mind and spirit are reunited, we find answers to the mysteries which draw back our hearts.

But how do we go about this vision quest? An ancient and traditional quest would have transpired over a period of four or more days, without food, clothing, or shelter, and often without water. In his legendary vision quest, Buddha found that the emancipative effects of such excess is not only unnecessary, but is precarious. Therefore the typical vision quest of today may only extend for a period of hours, or a day, with the benefit of water and shelter as desired.

The significant components of today's vision quest are: separation from the normal environment; finding a questing place out of direct range of human voices; staying out of the direct sight of other humans (although within range of sight and voice for security); and locating a place where the quester feels safe and secure, yet directly exposed to nature.

It is important to let the questing place choose you, rather than simply choosing a place of convenience. Some Indian tribes tie off the four corners (north, south, east, west) of an approximate three foot space, with tribal cloth flags, or colored prayer ties, representing the cardinal directions. For the Cherokee these tribal colors and corresponding cardinal directions are: white/south, red/east, blue/north, black/west. The time and effort placed into preparing for this ritual play a significant role in the vision quest experience.

"Let's sit down here, all of us, on the open prairie, where we can't see a highway or a fence. Let's have no blankets to sit on, but feel the ground with our bodies, the earth, the yielding shrubs. Let's have the grass for a mattress, experiencing its sharpness and its softness. Let us become like stones, plants, and trees. Let us be animals, think and feel like animals" (Lame Deer, 1972, p. 108).

There are two major formats for the vision quest. For both, I recommend taking a journal. One quest allows the participant to simply *be* in nature and take note of what is experienced—no plans. The other type, as documented by Bear Heart (1998), advises that one focus the meditation on three questions:

1. *Who am I?* All external identifications are to be redirected toward internal association—what do you believe, what do you stand for, what is your character?

2. *What have I become with the who that I am?* Are you using your God-given talents to serve others and grow as a person, or simply going through life doing what you wish?

3. *Why am I here?* What is the purpose for your life—not your work, not your goals, but your true inner purpose?

During the vision quest, journal your thoughts, your dreams, your visions, unusual happenings, and animals or anything else that is brought to your attention—no matter how insignificant it may seem. After a traditional vision quest, the quester will often discuss the quest with a holy man, or someone who might help interpret the meaning of that which was encountered.

One of the biggest mistakes made during a quest, a mistake which has been repeatedly shared with me, is that often the quester is seeking for answers through the *big things*, when it is the little things—a spider which continually draws the attention, a slow-moving cloud, etc—which often carry the message. We cannot force a vision or its meaning to come, we must simply allow it.

Communion with the Ancient Trees: There stands a virgin forest of trees, hundreds of years old, at the tip of the Laurel Falls Trail in the Great Smokey Mountains. As you gaze upon these magnificent chieftains of the forest, you are obliged to wonder at the stories they hold deep within their core. If they could speak, what would they have to say? And yet they do speak, if we but have the patience and insight to listen. Each tree has a lesson to share in it twisted limbs, in its gnarled bark, in the sound of its internal groans, or the way the wind spirits through its leaves.

Go into a forest or an area filled with trees and allow a specific tree to "speak to you." Carry a tree identification book and journal with you. Identify the tree and learn about it through the source book. Then learn what the tree has to teach you on its own. Write down anything that comes to mind or spirit. Don't take the time to determine whether it has meaning, simple "be" in the presence of nature and allow your thoughts to be governed by your environment.

Draw and journal about the tree's bark, colors, leaves, identifying markings, fruit, or anything growing on the tree. Journal its size, shape, width, sounds, smells, and textures—slowly allow its personality to present itself. Later in the day reflect back on your writings and appreciate what you have learned.

The Spirit-Ritual of Communion—the Circle:

"God's power is an expanding power. It is in the very nature of creativity that it shall grow, that it shall go from one stage to another stage. When any tree or plant ceases growing, it has already begun to die" (Sanford, 1982, p. 59).

The concept of communion is one of growth through intimate sharing of thoughts, feelings, beliefs, and faith. It requires a willingness to understand and support each other without fear of reprisal—what is shared with the group, stays with the group. If the group does not grow together, it dies together.

To most Native American tribes this idea of communion is symbolized by the circle—the circle representing the whole of the universe, including humankind and all other aspects of the creation. "You have noticed that everything an Indian does is in a circle, and that is because the Power of the World always works in circles, and everything tries to be round" (Black Elk, as told through John G. Neihardt, 1995, p 194). [Black Elk was an Oglala Sioux medicine man who suffered many of the atrocities directed toward Native Americans during the late 1800's and early 1900's].

To Native Americans the circle itself holds power because of what it represents. "When a group of Indians form a circle to pray, all know that the prayers have already begun with the representation of a circle. No words have yet been spoken and in some ceremonies no words need be spoken, but the intentional physicality of our formation has already expressed our prayer and deep concern for the wholeness of all of God's Creation" (Kidwell, Noley, & Tinker, 2001, p. 50). [Native American authors of *A Native American Theology*. They each represent different Indian tribes, coming together to draw some unified semblance of Native American spirituality, while maintaining the reality of quite diverse tribal beliefs].

The Talking Circle—the Talking Stick: The talking circle is a very common communion practice among a variety of Native American tribes. In this ritual, a talking stick (a ceremonially carved stick, from one to two feet in length and one to two inches in diameter), a ceremonial feather, or some other directional tool, or sacred item, is utilized to facilitate the flow of the group discussion.

A group leader takes the talking stick and shares information about the purpose for the day's talking circle and about himself. The directional implement is then passed around the circle, typically in a clockwise direction, although counterclockwise represents the spiritual to the Cherokee and the stick may, likewise, be so directed. I pass the stick around the circle four times, and on each round each individual is encouraged to share more information about himself, or ask for prayers or guidance. Only the person holding the talking stick may speak, so if a question, clarification, or other reply is desired, the stick must be handed to the one who wishes to share.

After a final pass of the talking stick, it is placed in the center of the circle and may be picked up by anyone who still wishes to have a word. Topics of discussion for a talking circle may be pre-determined or simply allowed to occur as directed by the group's needs and desires.

Pipe Ceremony: The Indian pipe ceremony presents a truly wonderful analogy for the spirit-ritual of communion represented by a circle and for the concept of the circle of life for all things created. There are various stories of how the sacred ceremonial pipe was originally brought to different tribes, but in each story it came at a time when there was great physical, mental, and spiritual need.

There are diverse representations for the components of the ceremonial pipe, but the one I most often use is as follows. The stem of the pipe is usually made of wood and may be up to a foot or two in length. The bowl is formed from clay or pipe stone. Special tobacco is prepared for the pipe ceremony. For the Cherokee it was called "remade tobacco" — tobacco that was ceremonially grown, blessed, and set apart for spiritual purposes. A ceremonial pipe is not smoked for pleasure, it is used for sacred rites.

The pipe bowl represents the universe. The tobacco represents all that was created which has life. And the stem represents man's relationship to, or connection with, the universe and all that was created. As the tobacco is lit, the smoke rising from the bowl represents the spirit-breathed prayers of mankind and the creation traveling upward to the Creator in praise, thanksgiving, offerings of service, and requests for blessings upon the creation.

As the ceremony is begun, tobacco is placed in the bowl as the pipe is directed toward each of the cardinal directions. Prayers are typically offered at each point, recognizing the meaning associated with each direction. *White/South*—represents birth, life, purity, new life, beginnings; *Red/East*—represents victory, power, success, strength, growth; *Blue/North*—represents illness, defeat, loss; and *Black/West*—represents death. These specific color/directional meanings are associated with the Cherokee—other tribes have differing color representations.

The pipe is then lit and passed around the circle, allowing each individual to draw smoke from the pipe, or to simply touch and pass the pipe on. As the smoke, representing the creation, is drawn into the mouth and mixes with the spirit-breath of man, the communion of the two then ascends together to the heavens. The individual holding the pipe may share a prayer, thankfulness, or a blessing before passing it on to the next person in the circle.

I have participated in a number of pipe ceremonies and am always impressed with the significant meaning the ceremony can have on all who take part in this spirit-ritual. *Physiologically*, the ceremony represents the unity of those within the circle with each other and with the creation. *Psychologically*, it is a visually reinforced image of active and effective prayers going forth to our Creator—a very important concept for visual learners. And *Spiritually*, the ritual allows the mind and spirit to unite.

Communion with Christ: "One of the wonderful things in the Catholic ritual is going to communion. There you are taught that this *is* the body and blood of the Savior. And you take it to you, and you turn inward, and there Christ is working within you" (Campbell, 1988, p. 61). Though most other Christian traditions do not see the wine and bread of communion as the *literal* blood and body of Christ, they do see it as a representation of such. In either case, the ceremony represents the unity of Christian to Christian and all Christians to God through a belief in the resurrected son—Jesus Christ. It is a public confession of belief and provides spiritual nourishment to the individual spirit and soul. "The Communion Service is not the only channel for receiving the life of God, but it is a very profound channel, involving symbolism that speaks not only to the conscious mind but also to the unconscious" (Sanford, A., 1983, p. 190).

"In the Christian tradition, Jesus does not demand a kind of perfection that we can accomplish on our own. He does say that we must be perfect, but adds the qualification, 'as my Father in heaven is perfect.' What does he mean by this? That when we are fused with him through Baptism and Holy Communion, we have taken upon ourselves *his* perfection. Consequently, when the Father looks down upon us, what he sees is the perfect Jesus, and when he blesses *him*, he blesses those who are within him" (Mails, 1988, p. 231).

In a story, as told by the Apostle Paul in First Corinthians, chapter eleven, followers of Christ had gathered together on the first day of the week to take part in this communion ceremony, or Lord's Supper. But in this story, those gathering together seemed to be more interested in their relationship to themselves than in their relationship to God and their fellow man. It is noted that some in the group did not get along with others in the group. Instead of waiting to take part in the ceremony together, as a communal rite, these individuals were simply eating and partying to the point of being "full and drunk" while around them the poor didn't even have enough to eat.

Paul's response (paraphrased): *When you come together as a church there is disharmony among you. There are groups within your community who are self-seeking in their desires and actions, which makes it obvious and easy to recognize those who are doing right.*

For when you come together you are not really eating the "Lord's Supper," you are simply filling your stomachs, for your own physical satisfaction. Why do I say this? Well, because when you eat, each person eats without waiting for the others — some people don't get enough to eat, while others not only get full, but they get drunk. If this meal is only about feeding yourself, don't you have your own houses to eat in? It seems to me that you think God's church, God's people, aren't as important as meeting your own selfish needs. Don't you realize you are embarrassing those people who are poor? If you don't like what I am saying, what do you think I should be saying to you — should I be praising you for doing this? No, I don't praise you.

The teaching I gave you is the same teaching that I received from the Lord. That on the night Jesus was going to be killed, he took bread and gave thanks for it. Then He divided the bread and said, "This is my body; it is for you, do this in remembrance of me" (NASB, 1995, I Corinthians 11:24) — it is for those who will represent the body of Christ once He is gone from this earth. Do this ceremony to remember Him and His body. Do this to proclaim the death and resurrection of the Christ.

Then He took the cup and said, "This cup is the new covenant in my blood, do this, as often as you drink it, in remembrance of me" (NASB, 1995, I Corinthians 11:25). It is to remind you of the binding agreement between God and his people. This new agreement began with the sacrificial blood, shed with the death of the Christ. When you drink this, do it to remember Him. Every time you eat this bread and drink this cup, every time you take part in this ceremony, you are making known, to those around you, the purpose of the Lord's death — that purpose being to bring all of mankind in unity/harmony under God the Father. Your actions will show this.

If, however, a person eats the bread or drinks the cup of the Lord in a way that is not worthy — if there is disharmony between himself and God and others — then that person is sinning against the body and the blood of the Lord; he is breaking a contract between God and himself, a contract signed by Jesus' blood and signed by himself the day he accepted Jesus.

You should, therefore, inspect yourself closely, test the condition of your heart and your motives before you eat the bread and drink the cup. For if you don't take the time to weigh the evidence for or against you — if you first don't make yourself right in the sight of God and others — you will surely feel the discipline and molding of the hand of God upon you. In fact this is the reason many of you are weak and sick, and some are even dead or dying. If you would simply take the time to examine yourself and get yourself right with God you would not be suffering so.

So then, my brothers and my sisters — my very special relationships in the Lord — when you come together, be in harmony, wait for each other, don't be so self-centered, but care about those around you. Do this so that your meetings together will make you strong, individually and as a group. Don't cause God to have to continually be disciplining you, but live your life in such a way that you will be a proclamation of your God.

So here is the spirit-meaning of the Communion Ceremony with Christ. This ceremony is a way for us to examine our relation to God, self, and others. It's not about eating crackers and drinking wine or juice as physical food. It is a Healing Ceremony. The foremost power is not the substance we take into our mouth — just like the primary power of baptism is not in the water — but the true power is coming to this ceremony, with a pure heart toward our relationship to God, self, and others. And if we cannot partake in the ceremony with a clean heart and pure motives, we are guided in Matthew 5:23 to go to our brother, or sister, or God, and make it right. Then we can truly take part in this ceremony. Then, and only then, can spiritual and physical healing take place. This ceremony is a "Big Deal." Its purpose is to influence us to keep our relationship chain whole. And the result? Our life will be healthier — physically, mentally, and spiritually (wellness) — beginning with our relationship to God, but overflowing to our relationship to ourselves and others.

Spirit-Rituals for Daily Activities:

"He is blessed who is assured that the animal is dying out in him day by day, and the divine being established" (Thoreau, 1965, p. 157).

Any activity can become a spirit-ritual by dedicating it to God, or a higher motive, and allowing the Creator to use us as vessels through which He accomplishes good. Such actions may be calls to spontaneous service, or regular daily activities.

For spontaneous calls to service, allow a need to present itself, dedicate your service in fulfilling that need to a higher purpose than self-fulfillment, let go of any attachments to pre-conceived ideas about the outcome of the service, then simply go and do it.

For regular daily activities, simply examine the holistic purpose for the pursuit—walking to exercise the body, relax the mind, and connect with God's creation; washing dishes to protect the family from germs and to keep the home neat and in order; mowing the grass to create beauty in God's creation; working to support the family; taking out the trash to remove physical and mental clutter; etc. Now, each time before beginning the activity take a deep breath, think about the higher purpose for the activity, consider all the senses involved, and concentrate on these during the endeavor—the sounds, emotions, textures, smells, colors, tastes, and the meaning the activity holds for your relationship to God, others, self, and the creation.

The Heyoka Spirit-Ritual:

"In the heyoka ceremony, everything is backwards, and it is planned that the people shall be made to feel jolly and happy first, so that it may be easier for the power to come to them. You have noticed that the truth comes into this world with two faces. One is sad with suffering, and the other laughs; but it is the same face, laughing or weeping" (Neihardt, 1995, pp. 188-189).

ASSERTION THREE

The Heyoka ritual is intended to get us in touch with our opposites. To participate, choose one or more activities and do them in reverse for a selected period of time—walk backwards, say no when you would say yes, when mad give a compliment, eat breakfast for supper, part your hair on the other side, say you are cold when you are hot, etc.

Through this ritual of opposites, we come to better understand the world around us and develop a better appreciation and tolerance for the manner in which different people operate, which is often totally opposite from the way we personally function.

The Spirit-Ritual of Offerings:

Jung (1957) asserts that our religious nature creates within us a call for offering. "Offerings are made to the invisible powers, formidable blessings are pronounced, and all kinds of solemn rites are performed" (p. 36).

Within each of us is a desire to make ceremonial offerings in admiration of our blessings. Dr. Jung notes that the nature of rationalists will deny this call, as well as any consideration in participating in the ceremonial activities which it evokes. Their outcry will be the words "magic and superstition" because they are incapable of pure psychological or spiritual insight, while at the same time they will use their own "magic and superstition" to support their opposing objectives.

Most Native American philosophies follow this same discourse of thought. And throughout time Native people have been judged (sometimes rightly, but often quite wrongly) as attempting to placate some angry deity with their rites and rituals. In Kidwell, Noley, & Tinker's research (2001), they found that more often these rituals are an individual's, or community's, means of connecting with the sacred "for the sake of the whole community" and a psychological methodology for reinforcing ethical responsibility (p. 41-44). This philosophy is also supported by Confucius in his belief that the following of tradition is the underpinning necessary for ethical behavior.

In other words, the physical symbols utilized in ritual and the following of traditions handed down throughout generations can psychologically, if not spiritually, assist the human mind in making a connection between the physical and spiritual. Sometimes these ritualistic traditions and symbols actually become the conduit between the two realms, while at other times they simply act as a psychosomatic reinforcement for current beliefs.

Bear Heart (1998) supports these findings and adds: "The missionaries thought our Indian people worshiped trees, eagles, the pipe, and many other things. We didn't then and we don't now—we are monotheistic. But we do acknowledge these things as gifts from the Creator, put here to help us. When we use herbs such as sage, cedar, and sweet-grass, we're not worshiping these items—we're using them to create an atmosphere where we feel comfortable addressing the Creator, whether we're in need of help or just want to adore His presence" (pp. 183-184). "If Native people are going to take something from it [the earth], be it herbs, a stone, or earth itself, we always give an offering, usually tobacco, in return. Then we gently take that herb or stone…and we pray that we will use it in a good manner" (p. 168).

Bear Heart goes on to declare that in making an offering and in giving thanks, we must honor and thank the Creator, noting that the Creator is the one we should revere by respecting His creation. He also follows with an interesting discourse: when the earth and her resources are used and ill-treated, without offerings, we will meet with the negative effects of natural disasters—earthquakes, hurricanes, etc. These negative affects of natural disasters are really the result of manmade things. Man is hurt or even killed by "slabs of concrete, collapsed highways, broken water mains, and gas lines"—all of his taking and making (pp. 168-169). When we learn to respect and show respect; when we understand that when we must take, we only take what we need; when we follow our action with prayer and offering, we will see a dramatic change in the outcome of the so-called whims of nature.

Kidwell, Noley, & Tinker (2001) call this inner plea to make offerings a "necessity for reciprocity" (p. 41). As an intricate part of the whole creation, there is something within us that compels us to reciprocate — when we take from the earth, as a product of the earth, we must give back. Whether it be the taking of plants for medicine, vegetables for food, wood for a fire, water for cleansing, or a human life during times of war, something within says to give back. And as noted by Bear Heart, if we avoid the call, we suffer the fall.

While most religious or spiritual movements do not support the idea of *superstitious* offerings to appease "angry gods" or idols, offerings in worship of the creation rather than the Creator, or the development of a psychological dependence upon any ritual, the concept of reciprocation through offerings is supported by all of the major religious and spiritual movements. We have simply changed the terminology, and rather than using the word *offering*, we *offer* a blessing or a gift.

Common offerings have been, and continue to be, a song, word, prayer, ring, wine, water, tobacco (and other plants), flour, grain, cinnamon, cane, oil, incense, cedar, smoke, fat, animal life, and other natural things that are a part of the creation or which represent the circle of life. While the sacrifice of some type of living being (typically animal life) was a part of most religious rituals at some point in recorded history, I find little support that this is a widespread practice today. For Christianity, it is believed that the ultimate blood sacrifice was made with the death of the Christ and no additional living sacrifices are necessary. As for Buddhists and Hindus, the sanctity of life requests non-violence toward all life — devout Hindus will therefore be vegetarians.

Blessings upon the Creation: It is seldom that mankind today offers a blessing upon the earth — the same earth which daily brings us our physical life and sustenance. An appropriate offering can be made at the riverside asking God to bless the waters to flow pure and clean to nourish all life with which it comes in contact. A blessing might be placed upon a piece of land on which a building or road is to be built. If a plant or other item is taken from nature, it is appropriate to offer thanks in some unique way. These rituals provide symbols to help us understand the blessings of the creation, offered to us by the Creator, and our relationship and responsibility to all that is created.

Prayer Ties: Many Native American tribes create prayer ties as a way to offer a blessing upon the creation. Small colored cloths, approximately 3″ x 3″ are cut, tobacco or other small offerings are placed at the center of the cloths, and the corners are drawn up into a small bundle and tied. Prayers are offered over the ties during the process or at its conclusion. These prayer ties are then left behind, hanging on a tree or any other chosen space. Or, the ties may be carried with the one who made them, or given to someone for whom a particular prayer is offered.

Prayer ties will often be red—symbolizing courage, success, victory, energy, or strength; or white—symbolizing purity, life, new life, or peace. The belief is that the prayer tie remains behind and continues as a request of the associated prayer, before the Creator, even after the one making the offering has gone. Much like the image of the smoke of a sacred pipe ceremony being carried before God, the visual image of creating a prayer tie provides positive reinforcement to anyone whose dominate style is as a visual learner.

As well as physical offerings, like tobacco, being placed within the prayer tie cloth, prayers may be written on the cloth and tied off in a similar manner as that used with a tobacco offering.

ASSERTION FOUR

Finding this key and beginning this journey is the only pathway to enlightenment. And bestowed upon the enlightened, is the gift of true fulfillment—authentic bliss.

"We must be willing to get rid of the life we've planned so as to have the life that is waiting for us" (Joseph Campbell as selected in Osbon, 1991, p. 18).

❖ ❖ ❖

Beyond the sacred veil are various levels of the spiritual realm—*level one* in which the spirit, or authenticity, of all physical entities reside while physical life still remains; *level two*, the place of disembodied spirits which once had physical life; *level three*, the spirit world of both good and evil (never physical) created spirits; and *level four*, the realm of the Supreme God. Within each of the levels there exist opposing planes (good and evil within the same level but on two opposing planes).

Man and nature, even within their spiritual authenticity in level one, are still separated from God by two overwhelming levels of isolation. But the light of God, from the highest plane, is made to shine upon man and the creation, penetrating through all levels and all planes with an almighty force and power. Only when the creation turns back toward its Creator, only when the key is turned, does the spiritual journey begin.

Religion (which typically begins as outward expression of service, purification, and consistency through mind/body ritual—*doing*), is meant to lead us to **Spirituality** (the internal growth and development of our spirit and soul where our service, purification, and ritual are generated from a sacred source, as a sacred service—*being*), which then shows us the pathway to **Enlightenment** (the inflowing of sacred light from level four, through level three and two, to level one, which then releases Godly wisdom and power, allowing us to see the inner beauty of all living things and empowering us to respond with sacred kindness and pure love—the highest of all motives). These sacred blessings of love and kindness then fill our entire being, from which they freely flow. And true enlightenment can only come from the Source (First Cause) of all light. It is this light, from the Creator of light, which consumes us, bringing with its brilliance, true fulfillment, joy—authentic bliss. To only open ourselves to spirit level two and three is a dangerous journey.

"It is not ethical principles, however lofty, or creeds, however orthodox, that lay the foundations for the freedom and autonomy of the individual, but simply and solely the empirical awareness, the incontrovertible experience of an intensely personal, reciprocal relationship between man and an extramundane authority which acts as a counterpoise to the world and its reason" (Jung, 1957, p. 32-33).

Sacred Service — A Call to Higher Motives

❖ ❖ ❖

"I am going to keep young in spite of the gray hairs; even if things do not always come my way I am going to live for others, and shed sunshine across the pathway of all I meet" (Marden, 1913, p. 244).

❖ ❖ ❖

"When it comes right down to it, we are nothing until that nothing becomes so dedicated that it is like a vessel through which good things can move, an instrument for receiving knowledge and sharing it with others who might be in need" (Bear Heart, 1998, p. 53).

Our sacred service is to be directed by our purpose — to take the gifts and talents with which we have been blessed, grow and expand these gifts and talents, and share these gifts and talents with others through our spirit in action. But what motivates us to share our gifts in service? For the *physically motivated* servant the goal is to receive something in return. For the *spirit-driven* servant, it is the pure joy of serving others. "I awoke and saw that life was service. I acted and behold, service was joy" (Rabindranath Tagore, as quoted by Walsh, 1999, p. 254). [Rabindranath Tagore was a Nobel Prize winning poet from India].

In the initial stages of becoming a servant it is acceptable to be directed by desires for reciprocation, for service in and of itself opens us up to spiritual connections. But as these spiritual connections are made, the servant should begin to operate from a different set of principles. We should be able to find joy in the little things, joy in the things we must do from day to day, joy in service. I have come to believe this is what Solomon, the great king of Jerusalem, spoke of in his wonderful Ecclesiastical discourse. In summary of his address:

- Enjoy life today—don't put off until tomorrow, or until you are old—for in so-doing, you may never find joy.
- Look for joy in the simple things—the things that you "must do" or with those you "must associate" every day—in eating, drinking, and working; with your spouse, your family, and your friends; and in service. See what needs to be done and do it. In such, you will find true joy; in such you will offer sacred service. If you cannot find joy in the simplicity of God's blessings and in serving others, you will not find it in grandeur or in being served.
- Learn to enjoy the walk, to enjoy the journey, and stop worrying about the destination. It is okay with God if you enjoy life's simple pleasures, because they are blessings from Him. A problem arises when *things* become more important than God and others. When it is all about me and what I want—the joy quickly fades.
- When life is good, enjoy it. When it is hard, remember that God gives us both good times and bad, happy and sad. But with God, we can make it through them all—each in its own time.
- Above all, love and respect God in all you do—obey His commands and enjoy His blessings. For even the secret things of man, He sees. He knows the good and the bad of our lives, and in the end He will judge us all for the servants we have become. Will we be judged as servants directed toward selfish desire, or servants directed toward our sacred service to others?

❖ ❖ ❖

How, then, do we create a desire toward sacred service? By accepting our role as vessels through which our Creator moves and operates in this world. Sacred service, like authentic love, comes as a gift from God. We all have access to it; some have simply suppressed it, denied it, or otherwise kept themselves from it through self-centered desires and fears—through lack of service. It seems that the more we want things for self, the less we wish to share them with others. And the more we hold on, the more fearful we become of letting go and serving. Until we connect—body with soul and spirit with mind—we cannot be faithful, sacred servants.

And how do we let go of the physical desires and connect with the spiritual? By beginning to see our service as a spiritual process that benefits others, and in understanding that in serving others we find spiritual growth. We let go by beginning to do everything we do as a spiritual practice. We stop dividing our lives into physical activities and spiritual activities, and we approach *everything* for a higher purpose—to serve God, others, self, or the creation. In so doing we find our purpose. Our purpose will be the product of our sacred service. As we see what needs to be done, we will just do it—for as God puts it before us, He also empowers us to fulfill the needs so presented. "Let man then learn the revelation of all nature and all thought to his heart; this, namely; that the Highest dwells with him; that the sources of nature are in his own mind, if the sentiment of duty is there" (Emerson, 1964, p. 276).

This aspect of sacred service is often overlooked. Even in the story of Jesus washing the disciple's feet, we time and again miss a vital component. The commonly derived lesson from this act of service is one of humility—no matter what our status, an appropriate ingredient in sacred service. What is overlooked is why Jesus chose to wash feet as His act of teaching the humility involved in sacred service. The reason? Their feet were dirty. True, pure, sacred service is about seeing that which needs to be done and taking it upon ourselves to do it. Service to others, for the benefit of others, is one of the most essential elements necessary for enlightenment.

Sacred Kindness—Finding Beauty in All Living Things

❖ ❖ ❖

"The greatest aim of life should be to absorb into one's being the largest amount of sweetness and beauty it is capable of absorbing" (Marden, 1913, p. 73).

❖ ❖ ❖

When a man sees a beautiful woman, he will most likely react with kindness in word and action. Though his response is one directed by desires for reciprocation, it is kindness none the less. As a man grows into a spiritual being, he will begin to see the beauty in all living things, and again he will react with kindness. But now his response is a spiritually automated reaction to the presence of sacred essence which pervades all life. "The salvation of the world consists in the salvation of the individual soul" (Jung, 1957, p. 69). As the inward man travels back to his source of being, he becomes driven in finding or recreating beauty in his environment.

"For we are a part of the earth and it is a part of us. The perfumed flowers are our sisters. The bear, the deer, the great eagle, these are our brothers...The rivers are our brothers. They quench our thirst. They carry our canoes and feed our children. So you must give to the rivers the kindness you would give any brother...Remember that the air is precious to us, that the air shares its spirit with all the life it supports . . . All things are connected like the blood which unites us all. Man did not weave the web of life, he is merely a strand in it. Whatever he does to the web, he does to himself. One thing we know: our God is also your God. The earth is precious to Him and to harm the earth is to heap contempt on its Creator" (Chief Seattle as selected in Jeffers, Susan, 1992). [Chief Seattle was of the Duwamish tribe, of the Northwest Nations—early to late

1800's. This speech was made before the Commissioner of Indian Affairs who wished to buy the lands of Chief Seattle's people].

Spiritual vision brings about an awareness of the inner beauty present in all things created, all things living. It allows us to see beyond the facade, into the spiritual essence. And it is at this level only that we see man, and the creation, as they were intended.

"Give me the man who, like Emerson, believes there is a remedy for every wrong, a satisfaction for every longing soul; the man who believes the best of everybody, and who sees beauty and loveliness where others see ugliness and disgust" (Marden, 1913, p. 232).

Why is it that when we see a tree all twisted and bent, we call it a thing of beauty, while noting the same characteristics in the human form as deformed and ugly? It is the way we have taught our mind to respond, but we can equally re-teach our mind by connecting with our spirit. Then, we can use our spirit-mind to find the inner-beauty in all living things.

In the beginning stages of this process, we may have to utilize the *Principle of Opposites* to visualize this beauty, but with dedicated practice, it should become automatic. "Think the good; drive away evil; keep the mind so filled with the good, the beautiful and the true, that the opposites will find no affinity there" (Marden, 1913, p. 233).

We can only begin to see the true essence and beauty when we look with our hearts and spirits, not with our simplistic minds. "Shall I not be as real as the things I see? If I am, I shall not fear to know them for what they are. Their essence is not less beautiful than their appearance, though it needs finer organs for its apprehension" (Emerson, 1964, p 225).

By now viewing life through the eyes of our spirit, we begin to understand that we are related to all living things—all living things are our family, all living things possess beauty.

"Brothers and sisters, continue to think about things that are good and worthy of praise. Think about the things that are true and honorable and right and pure and beautiful and respected. And do these things . . . and the God who gives peace will be with you" (Holy Bible, Easy to Read Version, 2000, Philippians 4:8–9). [Philippians was written around A.D. 61 by the Apostle Paul. At this time he was imprisoned in Rome. It was written to his friends and fellow Christians in the Philippi as encouragement and an expression of the joy to be found in Christ].

Pure Love For All Things Created

There is much ambiguity surrounding the word love. For one can love a car, a person, an animal, nature, money, food, or even evil. And love, in the eyes of the world, seems to come and go at its own beckoning. Often, this worldly love is nothing more than lesser emotions and chemical responses, and therein lies the disappointment and brokenness. In its highest form, love's stability becomes indisputably indestructible. Even a broken heart, a product of ill-advised love, eventually mends.

Unfortunately, the quest for love is much too often an escort on an erroneous journey—far too many hearts are left dispirited from this pilgrimage. We believe we are headed toward ecstasy, but the journey, and its destination, uncover only agony. What have we done so wrong? Why do we continue to miss out on love's grand promises? We miss out because we are looking for love on the wrong plane of existence.

Dr. Roger Walsh (1999) and Dr. Scott Peck (1978) say we have a false sense of what love is. We search and search outside ourselves for that select one, or the select few people, who will love us and for whom we can feel and show love. Some exhaust a lifetime in this desperate pursuit. We are driven to seek outside ourselves something we fail to provide within. We feel inadequate, deficient, and fearful, so we search outward to fill the void.

Yet, what we fail to understand is that until we heal our inner-spirit and soul, outward expressions of love will only bring temporary relief. We become attached, or even addicted, to other people—we must have their attention and approval. We make demands they cannot fulfill. We love them conditionally, yet refuse to accept their conditions for loving us. And we don't understand when this inappropriate concept of love fails, and why it hurts so badly. What we have mistakenly done is to confuse love with addiction. In reality, true love is based on wholeness—two wholes coming together as one, both giving 100%, not 50%. Two whole and separate units of spirit, soul, mind, and body declaring a mutually gratifying union: this is the true concept of love.

But where does this pure love come from, and how does it express itself? Remember when I spoke earlier of the vibrational effects of emotions? *Everything we physically do and say creates vibrations. These vibrations go out into the universe and affect those around us today and forever—from now into eternity. And any vibrations that go out, must first start their rhythm within: we are first and foremost affected by our thoughts and actions. The vibrations of good collect within and go forth to accomplish good without, opening doors to the sacred. The vibrations of evil collect and go forth to destroy, opening doors to the anti-sacred.*

The vibrational effects of love began with our Creator. After each creative effort, He stood back and said "It is good." In the beginning of time, the goodness and love of God went into all the creation, and the goodness and love of God flows outward still today. These sacred qualities are hidden with our spirit, awaiting an awakening. As we begin to take part in sacred service, as we begin to show kindness and recognize the beauty in all things living, we begin to feel the vibrational effects of their essence within our heart and soul. True, pure, spiritual love is a gift from God. No amount of trying to love on our own will provide its blessing. Only by opening ourselves up to the love of God, only by allowing God to work His blessings through us and in us, can we ever experience love in its ultimate capacity.

Throughout history the great religions and spiritual movements have praised love as the ultimate human quality. Both Jewish and Christian faiths tout it as the highest of all spiritual directives as does Hindu *bhakti* yoga.

Over two thousand years ago, when asked by a scribe to share the most important of all of God's commandments, Jesus answered: "And you shall love the Lord your God with all your Heart (spirit), and with all your Soul, and with all your Mind, and with all your Strength (body). The second is this, you shall love your neighbor as yourself. There is no other commandment greater than these" (NASB, 1995, Mark 12:30–31). [Mark was a disciple of Christ and probably the first to write a gospel account of the Messiah, around A.D. 55. This book was specifically written for a Roman audience]. Ghandi affirmed this belief and added that "every living being is your neighbor" (Ghandi, as quoted in, Walsh, 1999, p. 74). [Ghandi is one of the most recognized figures in the history of India. In the mid 1900's Ghandi became a symbol for nonviolence and peace around the world. His influence even played an active role in the civil rights movement within the United States].

In the Biblical story of creation, God, the Creator of all good things, created the heavens and the earth. On the sixth day, the Lord God formed man out of the dust from the earth. He breathed into man's nostrils the breath of life, and man became a living soul. In this creation process, I see God taking the soil He had created and forming the physical attributes of man—his body, his organs, his physical brain and blood—and we now know that these elements (elements from the soil) are present in our body in various mineral forms. So at this point there was a physical man (a physical body and physical mind), but he does not yet have life—these physical attributes have not yet been activated.

Then the Lord God "breathed the Breath of Life" into man—at this point He breathed man's spirit into him. And man "became a living soul"

(NASB, 1995, Genesis 2:7). The Spirit, the Soul, the Mind, and the Body were all a part of man as he was created by God, all a part of man as he takes care of himself (physically and spiritually), all a part of man as he finds meaning and purpose in life, and all to be given back to God and shared with His creation though the quality of love. The whole of man lies in the unity of these four elements. The ability to love lies in their interconnected harmony.

And how will we know this love? A true, spiritual love always makes the object of its affection feel important and special in its presence. Its ultimate desire is not to receive, but to give. Its goal is to awaken itself within the other—a love which is already there awaiting arousal. "It is a love expressed in the little things as well as the big: a note on the pillow; a call in the middle of the day; doing chores around the house; a kiss for no reason; an act of kindness or encouragement; or doing something we don't want to do but which needs to be done. Love always involves the expression of respect" (Hilliard, 2002, p. 102).

"True love doesn't require great financial investments, but is does require great personal ones. It is a love that does not come and go with the tide. Emotions may change, desires may adjust, but the love continues. True love is spirit-love. It does not come from the surface of our mind, but from the innermost chambers of our heart. It is unconditional—no strings attached. True love may or may not be accompanied by sexual attraction, but sexual attraction is not love" (Hilliard, 2002, p. 103).

Authentic love is the highest of all motives. It is the pinnacle of spiritual growth. For when man learns to love, his motives are so directed. His interpretation of the universe is reshaped to follow the pattern of his Maker. All within his presence, whether great or small, man or beast, are blessed. "If we love each other, then God's love has reached its goal—it is made perfect in us" (Holy Bible, Easy to Read Version, 2000, I John 4:12).

Authentic Bliss

"If you follow your bliss, you put yourself on a kind of track that has been there all the while, waiting for you, and the life that you ought to be living is the one you are living. Wherever you are—if you are following your bliss, you are enjoying that refreshment, that life within you, all the time" (Campbell, 1988, p. 91).

The phrase, "follow your bliss," was made extremely popular by the famous late mythologist Joseph Campbell. But the idea of following your bliss carries with it an assortment of interpretations from "doing whatever externally makes you happy" to "only finding happiness from within." In reality, there are aspects of meaning from both of these extremities.

The three phrases I will employ to describe authentic bliss are terms taken from Webster's New World Dictionary (2002): *Spiritual Joy*, *Heavenly Rapture*, and *Intense Pleasure and Satisfaction*.

Spiritual Joy:

"It is wicked to go about among one's fellow men with a face which indicates that life has been a disappointment to you instead of a glorious joy" (Marden, 1913, p. 229). But how does man overcome the despair of the world in order to allow his face to shine with the radiance of this glorious joy? By gaining insight into spiritual joy!

The word *spiritual*, first, denotes a connection with the inward person, not simply the physical shell or house within which the authentic person lives, but the innermost chambers of the spirit and soul. A second implication for the word spiritual involves a connection with the Spirit of the Divine. The Way of The Christ states that the Spirit of the Creator comes and indwells the spirit of the believer. This Divine Spirit acts upon the human spirit, which acts upon the human mind and body—in essence, the gift of *the* authentic Spirit Guide, directing, motivating, and caring for this entity we call man. The result—spiritual joy, a joy which sees the beauty in all living things, be they great or small. A joy expressed in sacred service and sacred kindness.

Man does not find this spiritual joy in the grandeur of life. Nor does he find it in those things which simply make him happy. For material things only bring about momentary pleasure. Rather, true joy is to be found in the simplicity of God's creation—the look of a child, moments of quiet serenity, a kind word. It is a joy found in these "little things." Things which are ordinary and seldom overwhelming in features, but they, none the less, excite the spirit and soul. And, in fact, it is not the "things" which bring the excitement, for that is only physical happiness, but it is an inward response to the Divine. It is spiritual essence, shining through the veil, which brings this bliss. "We may form this habit of happiness [spiritual joy] by making the most of little pleasures and not waiting for overwhelming joys" (Marden, 1913, pp. 153).

Heavenly Rapture:

A minimalist view of the word *heavenly* may simply depict what we visualize, or know to be, in the sky—the clouds, the winds, our atmospheric surroundings, and that which is above these air-filled entities. But viewed spiritually, the word also expresses the supposition of a heavenly or spiritual realm—an expanse of space beyond the physical understanding of the mind and beyond the physical confines of matter. Within my philosophy, this heavenly realm is a spiritual or metaphysical sphere or plane, within which there are several zones, or levels, each co-existing alongside the physical realm (revisit *Assertion One*). While our physical world is controlled by space and time, its opposite, the spiritual world, is not. Within the physical realm, we have physical limits. Within the spiritual realm, we have no limits—beyond those our physical being places on our spirit and soul.

In general, as physical beings, we live and operate on this side of a great veil between the two planes. This side of the veil is what we understand to be the physical realm. Earthly spirits of the creation, departed earthly spirits, unearthly spirits (angels, etc.), spiritual powers and authorities, and the Creator reside the other side of the veil, in various zones within the spiritual realm. But both sides are connected by the cosmic fabric of creation which acts as a network between each sphere and between each zone. This fabric allows for the transfer of communication and activity between the two realms.

At the dawn of existence, I believe these two realms were one, but with the fall of mankind, the two were split as opposites and will remain as such until the end of the physical world as we know it. But even though the two are split, there continues to be interaction between the spheres. In fact, many of our blessings, as well as our difficulties, are the result of powers that reside on the other side. "We are fighting against the spiritual powers of evil in the heavenly places" (Holy Bible, Easy to Read Version, 2000, Ephesians 6:12). The heavenly realm contains the presence of both good spirits and bad spirits, both God and Satan.

Now to the second word in this blissful phrase, heavenly rapture. *Rapture* signifies being carried away, lifted up, or transported, either body and/or soul; mind and/or spirit, into another realm.

Therefore, *heavenly rapture* necessitates a portion of our being, or its whole, to be pulled to a higher plane—to the other side of the veil. It follows to reason that it is within the realm of the heavenly that bliss will prove itself. Conclusion—authentic bliss comes as a gift from the other side of the veil, not from the physical realm. We must make this journey in order to find our meaning and purpose.

Intense Pleasure and Satisfaction:

There is an externally derived pleasure and peace that comes only when our environment is one of self satisfaction and serenity. Unfortunately, preserving egotistic contentment and ecological serenity are not common resources within the physical world. But, there is another type of pleasure and peace which transpires as tranquility of spirit—a peace beyond our psychological understanding. It is a peace which remains, even in the midst of turmoil. Intense pleasures often come in fleeing, momentary delights, but these pleasures are not sustainable. True pleasure is delight which sustains satisfaction. It is joyous contentment in whatever situation we find ourselves. A contentment based on a purpose-driven life of love and service. Therefore, the bliss generated from intense pleasure and satisfaction only befalls those with a spiritual resolve to fulfill their purpose—pure love expressed by sacred kindness and sacred service.

Conclusion:

To follow authentic bliss is to venture unflinchingly before the goal of your calling. To allow Divine intervention to indwell your spirit, moving you toward sacred service, allowing you to see beauty in all living things, to which your humble proportions respond with acts of kindness and love. As quickly as you can conform your life to this call of the spirit, the blessing of authentic bliss will begin to flow forth.

"The misery and the crime of the world rest upon the failure of human beings to understand that no man can be happy until he harmonizes with the best thing in him, with the divine and not the brute. The God within man is the only possible thing that can gain for him real happiness [authentic bliss]" (Marden, 1913, cover).

"If we can get God back into our souls, He will show us how to get back the joy of the earth, the pure joy of living upon it and the delight of serving it" (Sanford, A., 1983, p. 200).

ASSERTION FIVE

**Just as we can be led to true enlightenment,
true spirituality,
we can also be led astray.**

**"You will seek Me and find Me when you search for
Me with all your heart [the center of your spirit]"
(NASB, 1995—Jeremiah 29:13).**

❖ ❖ ❖

[The words of our Creator spoken through the prophet Jeremiah around 600 B.C.].

If you choose to take an authentic sacred journey it must lead beyond the sacred veil—it is there that you will meet God. Only from the Creator can the creation uncover its radiance. Only through our spirit can we encounter the Spirit of God.

"Don't believe every spirit. But test the spirits to see if they are from God" (Holy Bible, Easy to Read Version, 2000, I John 4:1). [John was the first cousin to Jesus. He also wrote the Gospel of John; two other letters, 2ND & 3RD John; and the great book of visions—Revelation. He was a gifted student in The Way of The Christ and a selected apostle. This letter was written around A.D. 90. Its purpose was to warn of false spiritual teachers and to counter Gnostic teaching which implies that "all that is of the spirit" is good and "all that is physical/matter" is evil].

One of the ways we can avoid pseudo-spirituality and test the spirits is by examining ancient sacred writings, the wisdom which throughout the ages has withstood the test of time. Within this book we have examined various ancient writings attempting to glean truth, where it might be found.

But the gleaning of truth is not always easy. Our spirit, just as it may hear the call of our Creator, may also hear the call of the world. And since we have been living in the world, walking at least in partial darkness, we might not have the illumination to appropriately interpret the source of the call or the message being delivered. Our spirit becomes slowly conditioned and darkened by the world, and turned toward the world. With these changes, our spirit may quite innocently lead us astray.

If we have not been walking day by day with the Creator in close communication, why should we think we have the ability to read the signs, to decipher the spiritual message? Also, we might be hearing the call of the Creator with our spirit and inappropriately deciphering the message with our worldly mind. Unless the spirit and mind are one, the message will always be clouded — reinforcing the necessity to begin with *Assertion One* before moving to the higher assertions.

Jung (1957) recognized this phenomenon of clouding as a "socio-political" movement of the world in which we live. For, if the individual is drawn toward religion and internal spirituality, he will lose his dependence on his external world and what it can "do for him" (p. 29). The world is then led to fear religion, which places a higher claim upon humankind than any man-made institution. In this state of fear, the world creates it own pseudo-religion, or in some cases holds to its claim in denying religion in any form. These views are then supported by a magnitude of false teachers going forth into the world, attempting to keep man confined in his corporal chains, while at the same time condemning all for which "true" religion upholds. The result for those attempting to follow the true path is often compromise of the spiritual, in order to keep from becoming estranged from the world. The negative vibratory effects of the world's fears are transferred to the believer. And the more fear and compromise, the more clouded our vision becomes.

The Apostle Peter, a personally selected disciple of The Way of The Christ, saw first hand the danger of these false teachers, as well as those who took the truth and perverted it into a "new religion" to meet personal desires and need. In A.D. 66 he wrote a letter which describes an eightfold pathway to true enlightenment, true spirituality, true religion, and then discussed the danger in becoming enticed by false spirituality. Peter goes on to state that those who do not follow the true path become blinded by the darkness of the world (NASB, 199, 2 Peter I: I-II).

To follow this pathway one must begin at the elementary stages of psycho/physio/spiritual growth, then "add to" each virtue, until enlightenment is attained. And in reality, enlightenment is never fully attained while encased within this physical mind and body, but it is a process of gaining insight (light) day by day. Slowly, as we move toward enlightenment, our spiritual cataracts are meta-surgically removed. As our vision clears, we finally see the pathway to God. Not a man-made image of God, not a synthetic movement with its altered motives, and not a cynical world view, but the authentic corridor through which we must pass to return to our Source.

Eightfold Pathway to Enlightenment

In *Assertion One* we established fundamental steps one and two:

1. Faith/Belief: We must first believe in the Spiritual Realm and The Source of All Things Spiritual, before we can take the sacred journey. Peter calls this The Way of the Messiah — The Way of The Christ. It is in this journey that we become partakers of the Divine Nature. Saint Thomas Aquinas (c. 1225-74), a scholastic philosopher schooled by the Benedictine monks of Monte Cassino and later a friar of the Dominican Order, stated: "Faith is a reasonable and virtuous state of mind because reason can show the propriety of accepting divine revelation" (Flew, Anthony, 1979, p.20).

For most people the beginning stage of faith is a faith passed on from parents. As we mature in both age and earthly knowledge, our beliefs will often be challenged and questioned. This is not a bad thing as some suppose, because an acquired faith is quite deficient until it is challenged—only through personal testing does faith become ours. Sometimes we will find ourselves as the man who brought his son to Jesus to be healed. When told "all things are possible to him who believes," the father cried out "I believe; help me with my unbelief" (NASB, 1995, Mark 9: 23-24). We are much the same. We have faith to a point, but to grow beyond requires Divine intervention.

Throughout this growth process we are often externally and internally encouraged to toss away the spiritual ways taught to us by our parents, church, or other leaders. I rather say we should only throw out those things which we find to be spiritually untrue, as we seek knowledge. And don't judge the spiritual teachings of these early mentors based on their performance—it is seldom we find a human, or a church for that matter, who/which consistently lives up to spiritual truth. But instead, work to understand the human condition as one in which free-will allows us to believe one thing and even teach it, yet sometimes fail to live up to its standard.

One might call this the faith of forgiveness. Dr. Scott Peck, psychologist and spiritual journeyman best known for his *Road Less Traveled* series, states it well: "Many of us have been harmed by religion. And when I talked about the necessity of forgiving your parents for the sins they committed in your childhood, I should have also said that it is equally important to forgive your church for the sins it may have committed in your childhood. Forgiving does not mean going back. I am not telling you to go back to the church of your childhood, any more than I would tell you to move back home with your parents. But your spiritual growth demands that you forgive nevertheless. Without such forgiveness you cannot begin to separate the true teachings of that church from its hypocrisy. And you need the true teachings" (Peck, Scott, 1993, p. 153).

2. Moral Excellence/Goodness: In its early stages, our faith will direct us toward moral excellence through the perceived need to accomplish good for the benefit of others, but we will still have frequent battles between our egoism and altruism. Often we must simply compel ourselves to do what is right in the face of fear or selfish desires.

Aristotle's viewpoint surfaced at this level, but he believed that it is in the presence of intellectual excellence that we are each drawn to moral excellence—through rational assessment we make choices about what should be done, not through faith (Flew, Anthony, 1979). But true spiritual growth must go beyond intellectual rational assessment. As our faith grows, it creates an apperception—an inward assessment and desire—to do good things by addressing our opposites for the greater good. We simply do what is right, even when our outward desires direct us otherwise. Since goodness is something we have little of, we begin to reflect the goodness of God. "We are all sculptors and painters, and our material is our own flesh and blood and bones. Any nobleness begins at once to refine a man's features, any meanness or sensuality to imbrute them" (Thoreau, 1965, p. 159).

In *Assertion Two* we discussed the need to move beyond our circle of worldly knowledge and understanding:

3. Spiritual Knowledge: As we do good for others, we stretch ourselves outside our circle, creating an atmosphere in which spiritual knowledge and understanding can flourish. We look outside of our circle and see a whole world opening up before us. We begin to understand more about God and spiritual phenomenon—not a worldly knowledge, but a spiritual wisdom which comes from the brief glimpses we witness beyond the sacred veil. We begin to create our own epistemology where a union of the physical and metaphysical are beheld—as we do things for others physically, we experience the reciprocal gift of spiritual knowledge.

4. Self-Control/Spirit Control: "Yet the spirit can for the time pervade and control every member and function of the body, and transmute what in form is the grossest sensuality into purity and devotion" (Thoreau, 1965, p. 157). As we gain spiritual knowledge and insight, we become empowered. Our spirit voluntarily places itself under the control of its Creator, and the Spirit of the Creator guides us in the resolution of conflict between our spirit, soul, mind, and body.

In *Assertion Three* we implemented the medium of spirit-ritual as the pathway to the sacred:

5. Perseverance/Patience: With self-control, spirit-control, comes the willpower and patience to be still and know God. In the fast-paced world in which we live, few take the time to slow down and experience the sacred. In reality, few take the time to "experience" anything. We simply do not have the necessary patience to exist as growing, flourishing, spiritual entities. Through sacred ritual we create an atmosphere where patience thrives. We are able to listen to holy directives and are no longer driven by what we want, when we want it. Ritual compels us to travel the path of patience. We must mentally and physically slow our pace during ritual, and in so doing we begin to gain tranquility of mind—the peace that is beyond our physical comprehension.

In *Assertion Four* we advanced to the higher callings:

6. Sacred Service: As we begin to understand the role ritual plays in our lives, we develop a Godly patience. Our service is no longer driven by *what we think we should do* or *what we want to do* but is now directed by a pure desire to serve God by doing what He has designed us to do—serve others. It is now our automatic response to serve and do good, without physical thought. We are so "full of God" that He simply flows through us to those around us—we act as a channel for spiritual energy. All of our service becomes sacred service; all of our activities become spiritual encounters. Our desire to serve not only transcends egoism, but it now transcends altruism as well—we now desire to help others, not for our sake or theirs, but without conscious thought; we just do what should be done.

7. Sacred Kindness: Our sacred service becomes obvious by the way we treat others. We see the beauty in all living things and recognize our relationship to the cosmos. There is no longer bitterness, hate, or anger, for kindness is now a "way of life." We become known for our random acts of kindness, even to those who labor to cause us harm. For we no longer see things for the actuality of what they are now, but we see them for the potentiality of what they can become. Sacred kindness is a supernatural reaction displayed in the presence of inward beauty. With holy eyes we see the reflection of the goodness of God in the creation. For when He spoke each life-form into being, did He not exclaim that "it is good"?

8. Pure Love: Our sacred kindness in appreciation for inward beauty leads to a pure love for God and all things created. A love for which we sacrifice self and become one with all living things. A perfect peace and harmony flows from us causing all others to feel important and loved in our presence. We become "like God," for "God is love." We don't become God, but our way of life, our entire being, expresses the love of God. Our spirit and mind are one. Our soul and body are one. And "we" are one with God and His creation.

❖ ❖ ❖

"Finally as awakening dawns and the separate self dissolves, any sense of personal striving, or doing, drops away—the seeker becomes a sage" (Walsh, 1999, p. 67).

❖ ❖ ❖

STAGE FIVE

The Journey Expressed

Spirituality — A Way of Life, Not a Movement

As amply expressed within the eightfold pathway, true spirituality, although many times directed through religious experience, is not about an organization, a movement, or a specific creed. Rather, it is a *Way of Life*. A life in which the spirit and soul are nourished, as well as the mind and body, as each entity learns its interconnectedness with the other. Then, as we become one with*in*, we learn to become one with*out*—one with those around us, as well as with all living things. All of our religious experiences become a manifestation of our spiritual qualities, for our spiritual qualities are now directed by pure motives. And with pure motives comes an openness to the true call of God. "Man flows at once to God when the channel of purity is open" (Thoreau, 1965, p. 157).

But just where will this flow lead us? This question is what keeps us from finding truth. We each have within us a desire to know our destination before we begin any journey. We want to latch onto a movement and follow its ways rather then seeking God and allowing Him to "move" us to a higher plane. I am not denying that there is a true path, but until we seek God instead of a movement, we will not find it. And if we have already begun a journey, the only way we can determine if we are indeed on the right path (with our current religious or philosophical beliefs) is to seek God through purity in motives. The directives within this entire treatise are intended, not to direct you to a movement, but to prepare you to encounter the Creator of your soul and allow Him, and Him only, to lay your path before you. And with this concept, we are exceptionally uncomfortable.

"The religious person…is accustomed to the thought of not being sole master in his own house. He believes that God, and not he himself, decides in the end. But how many of us would dare to let the will of God decide, and which of us would not feel embarrassed if he had to say how far the decision came from God himself" (Jung, 1957, pp. 98–99).

I had intended to present a great discourse into each of the major religious movements which have, throughout time, declared themselves as "the way." But through my research into each, I quickly determined that any one, alone, could encompass my entire manuscript. Throughout my studies, I was as amazed at the similarities in these religious movements as I was the differences, quickly supporting a previous conviction that each religion has been passed down with "bits" or "nuggets" of truth which were conceived from a First Cause, or a Central Truth. This truth is then modified, and in many causes vilely contaminated. Sometimes this adulteration has occurred with specific intent, but other times quite innocently, through years of oral and written tradition and by means of individual interpretation and translation.

This directs us to the concept of First Cause. First Cause implies that everything set in motion was put into motion, and all real things are brought about by a universal First Cause. And this cause is, in and of itself, its own cause.

Thomas Aquinas (1968) provides an excellent explanation of this process. "All things that are moved are moved by others, lower things by higher ones. The elements, for instance, are moved by the celestial bodies, and among the elements, the stronger move the weaker. Even among the celestial bodies, the lower ones are moved by the higher ones. Now, this procedure cannot go on to infinity. Since everything that is moved functions as a sort of instrument of the first mover, if there were no first mover, then whatever things are in motion would be simply instruments. Of course, if an infinite series of movers and things moved were possible, with no first mover, then the whole infinity of movers and things moved would be instruments. Now, it is ridiculous even to unlearned people, to suppose that instruments are moved but not by any principal agent. For, this would be like supposing that the construction of a box or bed could be accomplished by putting a saw or a hatchet to work without any carpenter to use them. Therefore, there must be a first mover existing above all—and this we call God" (pp. 158–159). Much of this concept of causative effect can also be seen in the works of Plato and Aristotle.

Aquinas also addressed the question of man's difficulty in believing that which cannot be seen. Religious leaders, spiritual leaders, and philosophers throughout the ages have underscored the human drive to seek after knowledge, therein substantiating the fact that man never receives complete knowledge, and will consequently continue to seek. If man within his limited wisdom could perfectly know all things, then it would be unwise and unnecessary to believe in that which he cannot see. But since man's intellect is so ineffectual, it becomes rather unwise to refuse to believe in the unseen, if further knowledge is to be gained.

Consider this fact: "If a man refused to believe anything unless he knew it himself, then it would be quite impossible to live in the world" (Aquinas, 1968, p. 286).

What child knows for a fact that his parents are his parents, that vegetables are good for us, or that George Washington was indeed one of our presidents. For us to exist in this world, we must believe *someone*. And if we must believe someone, why not the One who claims to be the source of all other someones.

What is the responsibility of one walking the road toward enlightenment?

There was a period, even during my lifetime, when I did not have to be able to defend my religious convictions, but that time has ended. The world is closing in on those who choose to follow after truth. As we are forced into the defensive mode we will either be absorbed into conformity, or we will rise to meet the external force. But if we keep our eyes to the path, if we follow the light, we have on our side the most powerful of all metaphysical collaboration. People do not truly come to God because we as men or women persuade or convince them that it is the thing to do. Rather, they hear the call of God, and they are moved inwardly—they are touched by God's Spirit. The power is not in the messenger. It is in God's power to touch, and man's willingness to hear and respond.

Yes, there are those who will never open their spirits to hear with an un-hardened heart, but we are not to be the judges of heart-pliability. We are to live the life and deliver the message. The energy of the Creator comes to us, and is channeled through us, so that we might truly see and hear God, and in so doing transmit His light to others. And as a man's or woman's soul is touched from beyond the sacred veil, it is then upon his or her inward being to listen and set a course of psycho/physio pursuit. "What does lie within our reach is the change in individuals who have, or create, an opportunity to influence others of like mind in their circle of acquaintance. I do not mean by persuading or preaching—I am thinking, rather, of the well-known fact that anyone who has insight into his own action, and has thus found access to the unconscious, involuntarily exercises an influence on his environment. It is an unintentional influence on the unconscious of others" (Jung, 1959, p. 121).

My Journey

I was blessed with loving parents, and though they were conservative Christians, they did not manipulatively force their ideals on me. Rather, I saw in their lives that they indeed lived their beliefs and were blessed for such living. They presented me weekly, if not daily, with opportunities for spiritual growth. Such a family heritage is a blessing with which many are not privileged. For those without such a spiritual upbringing, the journey might, at times, seem insurmountable. But it is not, for if with earthly parents we were not blessed, a heavenly relation we each can embrace.

For me to believe in a Supreme God, the Father and Creator of all that lives, was never of difficulty. Indeed, the creation has always seemed to shout, at every turn, the name of her Source. The earth and her possessions appear to me as the narrative of a Supreme existence — they are His story and within each and every element lay a portion of His divine and mysterious nature. This Supreme God is the beginning and the end. The creation is the chronicle in-between. If I was to know the Maker, I was to read His story.

So I first came to know God through my parents, but soon thereafter learned to "experience" God through His story of creation, a story read to me many times by both my mother and father. But I speak not simply of a written story, but rather a living story, as spoken by the wind, or a boisterous stream. "The simplest and oldest way, then, in which God manifests Himself is not through people but through and in the earth itself. And He still speaks to us through the earth and the sea, the birds of the air and the little living creatures upon the earth, if we can but quiet ourselves to listen" (Sanford, 1982, p. 22).

Through my experiential treks into nature I came to believe that if man was a product of a Creator, the creation, in a state of purity, would have to recognize its source. My spirit, if it could be renewed, sustained the capability of knowing its Creator. And once this knowledge could be found, anything less than being reunited with the source of being, would be a meager substitute for the right of entry into being re-made into perfection by the Master Artist of creation. Any alternate course would simply modify my being; it could not regenerate me into a complete and perfect entity—that for which I sought. I then came to realize that any man-made spiritual movement was merely an alternate course, not a true path. For authentic truth, I was to look to the Source of Truth. Movements only possess pieces of truth. "Whatever exists by virtue of another being may be traced back to a cause that exists by virtue of itself" (Aquinas, 1968, p. 291). I must get back to the First Cause.

But a belief in this First Cause—God—was found to be represented by a physical world view which embodied a multiplicity of concepts and passageways—movements. My journey continued. My travels have led me to ministers, monks, and medicine men. The similarities I have found within these and other movements have led me to my belief that they each point back to that Source, but that under the leadership of mere men, they each have faltered in their advance. God would surely not leave it up to fallen man to spread His truth upon the earth. He must come and share His truth in person.

What among the similar teachings of the spiritual movements shared this view? I then found the *Principle of Opposites and Similars*. If the rule of opposites has been in existence since the creation, then the opposite of God in spiritual form, is God in physical form. Therefore, God, in continuing the Principle of Opposites He established, had to extend Himself to man in physical form (His opposite) in order to bring man to his opposite (spiritual form) so they once again could be re-formed as similars, thus allowing for God and His creation to return to Oneness. And unlike any of the other religions or philosophies, I found that The Way of The Christ holds at its core a God who came in human form to guide man home. Had I found my truth, or just another movement?

As I examined each of the major religious movements I found one fairly common belief—that Jesus Christ was indeed an exceedingly spiritual being; that He still has a spiritual presence today; and that He was either a direct manifestation of the Creator as God in the flesh, or at the bare minimum an inspired messenger for God. None of the movements of which I studied denied His existence or power. And I found, in no other belief system, a personal God like the one declared by The Way of The Christ. A God who would give up an aspect of his Godhood to come to earth, to live and suffer as a man, so that man could be re-made to be like Him.

The Way of The Christ—Christianity: For centuries kings have sent their word out into the kingdom stamped with their seal as proof of the message. The Way of The Christ is described as such. For He came speaking the word of the King. He declared Himself to be the Son of the King. He carried the seal of the Holy Spirit of the King—which was first made manifest upon Him in the form of a Dove at His baptism. He came representing the power of the King through a multiplicity of documented miracles. This Messiah was deemed not as a movement leader, but as the source of movement—He was declared as God in the flesh. If The Way of The Christ simply points to a spiritually thinking man, it is simply a movement and is partial truth. But, if it authentically points to God, it is truth.

Unfortunately, much of what has been declared as the Christian message since the time of Christ has simply been a "movement" and has not been firmly based upon its Source. Too many Christians today are merely *physical Christians* and have no comprehension of how to become a *spiritual Christian*—a true follower of The Way of The Christ.

The name Christian was originally given to those who accepted The Way of The Christ, confessing this Jesus as the Messiah—as God in the flesh. If this was God in the flesh, these early Christians were following

First Cause—they were following God, not man. And today, over 2000 years later, we would do well to follow First Cause and not allow ourselves to get caught up in any manmade movement.

But how does one follow The Way of The Christ yet not follow (get caught up in) a movement? *The Way* means the path or the journey. *Of* means to come from or in union with. *The Christ* can be interpreted as the Messiah, the Chosen One, or even Creator. To follow this Way, we are to return to our Creator along our chosen path—the path that will unite us with the One from whom we came. We are made from the Spirit, the energy, of God our Creator. And we are to return to that energy. We regain that energy by becoming "hidden with Christ in God" (Colossians 3:3)—by *becoming* the Way of The Christ. We don't simply *follow* the Way: we *merge* with it. We *become* the Way of The Christ as we accept Him and allow Him to work in us and through us.

Christianity is the only spiritual methodology I studied which not only presents a directive for human thought and action, but where the Creator, Himself, comes and indwells the creation (humankind) providing the power to follow through with what should be done.

Throughout history God has blessed those peoples and countries that follow after Him, and He has cursed and destroyed those who have followed after movements. For our wonderful country to continue to receive the blessings of God, we must be a people who believe in, respect, and follow after our Creator. We must be a people who unite ourselves with God. We must give up our idol worship of movements and return to our Source.

What authentic Christianity does for me is bring harmony to all these other religions and philosophies. It has touched my heart as the place where truth is discerned and revealed. I admit, it does not answer all the questions to the mystery of life, but then where would the mystic be without unresolved mystery; where would the explorer be without a future journey? Some answers will be held until we meet God face to face.

If Christ was not God, than Christianity is simply a movement, and I find that all movements fall short of our divine destination. But if, indeed, Christ was God—our Creator revealed in the flesh—then Christianity is our journey home. Rather than a mere movement, it *is* the aboriginal voyage we all seek.

STAGE SIX

Major Spiritual Movements

The major religions of the world are typically defined within two principal categories. Those which are polytheistic (believe in many gods) and those who are monotheistic (believe in only one god). Most of the eastern religions fall in the first category: Hinduism, Buddhism, Taoism, and Confucianism. The western religions typically believe in one God: Islam, Judaism, and Christianity. Native American and philosophical beliefs tend to differ from tribe to tribe or philosopher to philosopher, although most of my research finds an overall belief in one superior being who created the world, with many tribes/philosophers expressing themselves as totally monotheistic. Likewise, it also appears that those declared as polytheistic seem to reference one superior power even if they believe in many.

Joseph Campbell (1988) states that the western spiritual aim and ideal "is in living the life that is potential in you and was never in anyone else as a possibility . . . that each of us is a completely unique creature and that, if we are ever to give any gift the world, it will have to come out of our own experience and fulfillment of our own potentialities, not someone else's" (p. 151). He then counters this with an eastern spiritual view in which "the individual is cookie-molded. His duties are put upon him in exact and precise terms, and there's no way of breaking out from them. When you go to a guru to be guided on the spiritual way, he knows just where you are on the traditional path, just where you have to go next, just what you must do to get there. He'll give you his picture to wear, so you can be like him. That wouldn't be a proper Western pedagogical way of guidance" (p. 151).

[My major source of information concerning Hinduism, Buddhism, Taoism, Confucianism, Islam, and Judaism was the wonderful book, *The World's Religions,* by Huston Smith, 1991].

Hinduism:

The followers of Hinduism believe this movement to be the oldest of religions, going back over 4000 years, but since documented writings only go back a few hundred years B.C., it is impossible to determine its true date of origin (Life, 1957).

Much of what we think about Hinduism surrounds the concept of self denial, although this is not an entirely accurate portrayal. For if pleasure and success are the direction a Hindu feels he should follow, then follow he may. Maybe even the pathway of desire is what leads to a longing for something more worthwhile. But the Hindu must also realize that if his life never extends beyond this elemental path of physical desire, further goals may not be realized.

And what is it the Hindu seeks? Infinity—infinite being, infinite knowledge, infinite bliss and joy. Hinduism says these blessings are ours to take hold of; they are within, waiting on us to retrieve them. They are God in the hidden self. They are Brahman, the Divine One, the Absolute—the pinnacle of oneness. The goal is to pass beyond the physical self of imperfection through detachment of worldly things, and be joined with God. This goal requires the ability to see all things living as one, all things living as striving to return to oneness.

In Hinduism, the pathway one must follow to achieve this goal comes by means of a term we associate with an eastern exercise practice—yoga.

The traditional word *yoga*, however, transcends far beyond this simplistic understanding. It means to discipline oneself, through practice and training, into a union of the physical and spiritual attributes of humankind—to physio/psycho/spiritually connect with the God within. Hinduism notes four distinct journeys, with a separate yoga method directing each path.

The first yoga pathway is called *Jnana yoga*. This practice begins by learning from spirituals leaders, but then excels beyond instruction to intuitive thinking and reflection. Then lastly, as one grows in the discipline, a state of persistently operating on a spiritual level is obtained.

Bhakti yoga—"The aim of bhakti yoga is to direct toward God the love that lies at the base of every heart" (Smith, 1991, p. 32). While the Jnana yogi's goal is to join with God, the Bhakti yogi's goal is to love and adore God with one's entire being and with no ulterior motives.

And how does one love a God that cannot be physically seen? Many Hindus say that at this stage enter the myths, symbols, and hundreds of images representing God. The symbols often noted are not meant to be the actual life-form of God, but simply various representations of the concept of God—images to touch and motivate the human senses.

Are the Hindu, then, idolaters and polytheistic, or are they merely presenting their individual understanding of God through a variety of images? It depends on who you ask, be they Hindu or not, and whether or not the practice of utilizing graven images is acceptable to God.

The third yoga pathway, *Karma yoga*, is the way of work. By finding meaning in everyday activities—the things one must do—meaning in life is also found: God is found. Work becomes more than a simple activity in which one must daily participate. Rather, through work, humankind can transcend the physical plane by partaking in this daily activity as a sacred experience.

The fourth yoga, *Raja yoga*, is a pathway of psycho/physio practices, or exercises, which are intended to connect the physical mind and body with the spirit. Meditative practices are a premier part of Raja. To the Hindu, spirituality literally means to return to the spirit. Raja yoga is meant to provide a pathway for this to occur.

The Hindu belief in God accepts two differing views: God as a personal God, similar to the Christian view, and God as transpersonal. As a personal God, He is the Creator *(Brahma)*, Preserver *(Vishnu)*, and Destroyer *(Shiva)*. Or as a transpersonal God, He started everything into motion and now stands back and allows the creation to follow its course.

My final topic relating to the Hindu movement is reincarnation. Hinduism sees the soul as entering the world through God. The soul begins in a simple life-form, but with the death of that life-form, the soul continues in another life-form. It transfers from one body-form to another, increasing in complexity with each transfer until reaching a human body-form. Then, "the career of a soul as it threads its course through innumerable human bodies is guided by its choices, which are controlled by what the soul wants and wills at each stage of the journey" (Smith, 1991, p 65).

This belief follows that the spirit and soul may be guided by God or the call of the world. If and when it is totally guided by God, the reincarnation process ceases and man and God have become one. In this final stage the soul either loses all association with its past and is completely identified with God, or it forever rests alongside God.

Buddhism:

Buddhism originated as a protest against many of the corruptions of Hinduism, especially in its treatment of people. It began with Siddhartha Gautama of the Sakyas. He was born in 563 B.C., the son of one of the many kings of provinces of India. He grew up with wealth and luxury, sheltered from the poverty, pain, and suffering of the surrounding kingdom.

In his 20's Gautama became discontented with his shallow life and ventured out into the real world for the first time. Upon this adventure, he encountered the way in which the common man, woman, and child lived and died, and for years this inconsistency between his life and the life of the real-world laid heavy upon his mind. In his 29th year, Gautama shaved his head, clothed himself in simple dress, and left forever his former life, including his wife and son. His journey, thereafter, became one of seeking after truth.

For a period of time Gautama studied Raga yoga and Hindu philosophy. He then followed these studies with a phase of excessive self-body discipline, taking so little food that he eventually became weak almost unto death. This experience was in direct opposition to his upbringing of excessiveness as the son of a king, and was said to have taught him the futility of extremes. Out of this life lesson came his illustrious principle of "the middle way."

In the next phase of Gautama's journey he devoted himself to thought and reflection into the mystery of life. It was during this juncture that he one day sat down below a tree and vowed not to arise until he had reached enlightenment. And it was from below this tree he arose to become known as "the awakened one" or "Buddha."

During the following forty-six years, Buddha traveled throughout India preaching his message. Many touted him as a god, though he never claimed such a position himself. The message he proclaimed was a challenge to avoid becoming controlled by human authorities and institutionalized religious movements, and in their place to seek after truth, a personal religion, and enlightenment. Buddha condemned the misuse of rituals and tradition as becoming nothing more than superstitious rites to false gods. He believed this misguided action hindered man's spiritual growth and blocked his vision from authentic truth. He further believed that superstition and an obsession with the supernatural prevented man from attending to the work that was presented before him everyday.

The sum of Buddha's teachings is found in what are classified as the **"Four Noble Truths:"**

1. Life is full of suffering and pain.
2. Suffering and pain are caused by our selfish desires.
3. The cure for suffering and pain is to let go of selfish desires.
4. We can let go of these desires by building positive relationships and through appropriate spiritual discipline.

These spiritual disciplines are best described in Buddha's **"Eightfold Pathway:"**

1. **Right Views:** "A way of life always involves more than beliefs, but it can never bypass them completely" (Smith, 1991, p. 104).
2. **Right Intent:** There must be a higher motive behind all others. Buddhism places enlightenment as the highest.
3. **Right Speech:** Do we speak the truth? Do we speak kindness and love? Do we speak to build up or to tear down? We must speak with purpose.
4. **Right Conduct:** What are the motives for what we do? Are our behaviors appropriate for a truth seeker? We must act in accordance with our spirit.
5. **Right Livelihood:** Is our work, our vocation, a part of our calling? Does it support an appropriate way of life? Is our job an outgrowth of our true self, or are we inappropriately becoming an outgrowth of our job? We must be able to be our true selves in the work we do.
6. **Right Effort:** There is great power in the inner-will of man. We can become strengthened and empowered by this drive, or slowly overtaken by the draw of the world.
7. **Right Mindfulness:** What do we put into our mind and how do we make use of its qualities? How do we transfer our

thoughts into action? And do we have control over our mind, or does it control us? We must learn the art of meditative mind control.

8. **Right Concentration:** We must practice techniques which bring about the physio/spiritual connection of our physical and spiritual qualities.

Buddhism believes that as we follow the Eightfold Pathway, we develop the spiritual desire and ability to let go of our physical attachments, which then brings about the bliss of enlightenment and eventually Nirvana—the extinguishing of our physical boundaries as we enter a state of spirit-life.

While Buddhism officially claims no belief in God, there are many similarities in its views of purpose, enlightenment, and Nirvana, with that of spiritual movements believing in a Supreme God. And even Buddha spoke of a non-created, non-born, spiritual form and an eventual delivery from our physical form.

Confucianism and Taoism:

The way of opposites reminds me of Confucianism, with its social and individual order. Taoism reminds me of the more natural way that should result as one matures in the way of spirituality—"the way"—known as Tao. To me, it seems that both philosophies carry value in the journey of mankind, in that social and personal order tend to lead to an opening of the spirit, and an opening of the spirit leads to social and personal order. Taoism's opposite (though not a negative opposite) is Confucianism. They must interlock in creating true Tao.

Confucianism: Confucius—Kung Fu-tzu—was born in China in 551 B.C. His father died before Confucius turned three, and he was raised in poverty by his mother. It was probably this upbringing that made him understand and become a proponent for the common man and woman.

While he never considered himself a sage, he was indeed a great teacher—usually teaching in informal settings and addressing problems and concerns of the day.

The major teachings of Confucius supported social order and the deliberate following of traditions. He believed that disorder in the world was a by-product of the loss of traditions. These traditions, as he viewed them, provide a road map for our individual journeys—laying out the pathway, within our specific culture, for individual beliefs and behaviors. Confucius held the conviction that people must study correct attitudes and behaviors both formally and informally. Moral thought and action should be taught, and practiced, until they become habit. Life must have a pattern, and man must seek and find that pattern and follow its strategies.

Confucius called for people everywhere to show love, express goodness, and earn and convey an attitude of humility and respect. His teachings sought after order by serving others with their well-being in mind; following a prescribed way of life full of ritual; leading others by good moral example; and valuing the aesthetic, cultural, and spiritual beauty in all things living and in all things representing life—music, poetry, literature, visual and performing arts, etc.

While Confucius spoke little of the spirit-world, he personally acknowledged his call as a request from heaven to teach, and he gave his entire life in this effort. It was a call to bring unity between man and heaven, unity between the earth and her Creator. This call directs man to become fully human—not human as is evidenced through self-centeredness, but humanness which transcends earth and touches heaven. A spirit-directed human, as the heavens appointed man to be.

Taoism: Taoism (pronounced Dowism) originated with Lao Tzu, assumed to be born in China around 604 B.C. Many questions surround Lao Tzu, beginning with whether or not he actually existed, or if he only existed through myth and legend. Secondly, we do not know his true name, for Lao Tzu is a term of endearment meaning "Grand Old Master." And thirdly, his major writings entitled "The Way"—the basis text for Taoism—seems to come from nowhere and appears to be written by more than one person.

The word Taoism was given to the Lao Tzu movement because *Tao* means "The Way"—the way of spiritual reality beyond the physical plane, the way of the universe and its spiritual flow of energy, and the way of human life as it joins with the Tao of this universal spiritual energy.

Taoism has at least three approaches to finding The Way. Philosophical Taoism involves self-motivated training—"to live wisely, the Taoist philosophers argued, is to live in a way that conserves life's vitality by not expending it in useless, draining ways, the chief of which are friction and conflict (Smith, 1991, p. 200). The method for doing so? *We wei*—supreme effortless activity and relaxation. To relax the conscious mind, and body, thus allowing spiritual power and energy to flow into and through you—directing this energy into appropriate action.

Religious Taoism, or Church Taoism, institutionalizes Taoist activity into a list of supernatural rituals which it follows precisely. Close adherence to these activities is believed to bring spiritual energy and healing to its followers.

The third form of Taoism involves the release of *Chi*—a vital flow of energy. By increasing the flow of this energy into and out of our mind and body, we find healing. This process begins by a personal, ritualistic cleansing of the mind and body by releasing worry and earthly distractions—letting go of attachments. Any activity can, then, ultimately open one up to the pure flow of Chi—eating, exercising, meditating, working. The key? A holistic approach to the activity, where the spirit, soul, mind, and body are each properly activated and participate in unison. Opposites are to find unity; yin and yang concepts are to interact.

Taoism also recognizes the spiritual quality in nature, seeking to join forces between man and nature, rather than dominating and conquering. A Taoist approach is an environmentally friendly approach to everything we do.

Philosophical Beliefs:

While most religious and spiritual movements are based on a faith, or belief, in a Supreme God, or Gods, after which their teachings follow, philosophers attempt to find grounds for defending a belief in God through reason and logic. Many philosophers feel it is man's destiny to do so, believing that an understanding of God and His existence is imperative to a positive life experience. Then there are "religious philosophers," who proclaim that spiritual knowledge may be supported by both faith and knowledge. It is in this realm of philosophers I fall.

Among my favorite philosophers is Ralph Waldo Emerson, who sees God as an "Over-Soul," or the metaphysical energy source behind all other life-forms (souls). "The philosophy of six thousand years has not searched the chambers and magazines of the soul. In its experiments there has always remained, in the last analysis, a residuum it could not resolve. Man is a stream whose source is hidden. Our being is descending into us from we know not whence...I am constrained every moment to acknowledge a higher origin for events than the will I call mine...that Over-Soul, within which every man's particular being is contained and made one with all other. We live in succession, in division, in parts, in particles. Meantime, within man, is the soul of the whole; the wise silence; the universal beauty, to which every part and particle is equally related; the eternal One" (Emerson, 1964, p. 262).

I believe Emerson shares an almost universal philosophical belief, that there is something for which we all seek, something greater than the simple finite which is visible to the physical eye. A metaphysical First Cause, which/who is accessible to all who search within the depths of the individual heart—a heart, which is in some way, is connected to all other hearts, all other souls, and the Creator of all that has life.

Native American Beliefs:

Spiritual beliefs, beginning with Creation stories among Native American tribes, are as varied as the tribes themselves. There are, however, three major cosmological views of human beginnings: people formed from the dust of the earth, people emerging from below the surface of the earth, or people coming down from above. In each instance, the action of a Supreme Being is manifested through previous creation.

James Adair (1775) concluded that the southeastern Indians, including the Cherokee, are descended from the Hebrew or Jewish race, which, in his mind, perpetuated many customs which seem distinctly Jewish in form.

J.H. Payne (N.D.) also noted these similarities as well as those resembling the Christian faith. According to his research, the traditional Cherokee believed in one Supreme Being, a God and King who appeared on earth for a time and was known as *Ye Ho waah*—the Hebrew and Christian God is called YHWH or YAHWEH. [John Howard Payne (1791–1852) lived among the Cherokee and worked intensely to resolve many of their political and governmental difficulties. His manuscripts, *The John Howard Payne Papers*, are recognized as one of the best documented sources of Cherokee history and antiquities in collected data].

Timberlake (1927—from his memoirs of 1756–1765), Adair (1775), and many other authorities of this time period support claims that the Cherokee, and many of the other Southeastern tribes, worshiped one Supreme God and were not given to idolatry. Mooney (1891), however, believed that the religion of the Cherokee was Zoo-theistic in that they worshiped animals and nature. [Timberlake was another man, who like Adair, lived among and studied the Cherokee people in the mid 1700's].

Archie Sam, born of the Cherokee Nation in Oklahoma, in June 30, 1914; chief of the Medicine Spring dance ground; and son of White Tobacco Sam of the Bear Clan (a Natchez-Creek Indian) and Aggie Cumsey Sam (a Cherokee Long-Hair), shares well the spiritual beliefs of the Cherokee in the following portion of his speech of 1976, at the University of Oklahoma. "A long, long time ago a messenger from heaven came to live among the Indians. He was a kind and humble man. We knew he was from heaven and not one of us because he would shine in the dark. He said his message from heaven was that Indians should care for and help one another, that Indians should live by the word of God, and that if they did they would be blessed with a happy life. He told the Indians about man's relation to nature. Earth was God's creation, and man was put here to take care of it. The trees, rivers, mountains, flowers, and animals are part of God's design, and man should preserve it for the coming generations to enjoy" (Mails, 1996, pp. 326–328). Through my dissertation research, I have found that the Cherokee of today (Eastern Band of the Cherokee) still widely accept this view of spirituality and by and large recognize Christianity as the methodology for approaching the Creator. It can likewise be stated that many other tribes do not accept this view.

"Indian spirituality is characteristically oriented towards balancing of the world and our participation in it both in everyday personal and family actions and the periodic ceremonies of clans, societies, and whole communities" (Kidwell, Noley, & Tinker, 2001, p. 41). While early Native Americans seemed to handle well this balancing act of spiritual and physical, mainly viewing all of life as spiritual in essence, Campbell (1988) claims that many of today's spiritual movements, especially those of the west, in their attempt to meet social needs and demands, are overlooking the obvious importance of a religion which seeks after the mystery of life—after the spirit and soul. Thus the draw toward spiritual movements like Native American and Eastern traditions, which search for a mystical experience.

Judaism, Islam, and Christianity:

To understand Christianity, Judaism, and Islam, we must understand that they each trace their roots back to Abraham. Some of the earliest of Old Testament history, through Moses, tells us that the God of Creation made a sacred covenant with Abraham and his descendents (Genesis 17).

Abraham's sons were Ishmael (with his maid-servant Hagar) and Isaac (with his wife Sarah). The Islamic people are genetic descendents of Ishmael. Though much of the history of the descendents of Ishmael has been lost, we know that God placed a blessing upon them—they would become a great nation (Genesis 21:13). The Jewish people are genetic descendents of Isaac (called God's son of promise)—though a blessing was placed on Ishmael, Isaac is noted as the "only heir" of Abraham in Genesis 21:12.

Isaac had two sons, Jacob and Esau. Upon his death, Abraham passed on a spiritual blessing (his covenant blessing) to Jacob (Genesis 27: 27–29). Jacob (later named Israel by God) had twelve sons who formed the twelve tribes of Israel. Much of the heritage information about the descendents of Isaac's tribes other than Judah and Levi has been lost.

The covenant from God to Abraham was later reaffirmed with one of Abraham's descendents through Jacob—David, King of Judah and Israel. These people would have been the People of Israel or the People of The Covenant. Their tribal descendents would be the ones we now recognize as Jews.

Originally the term Jew was a word applied (probably by those who were not of Jacob and David's decent) to those who inhabited the land of Judah (known as *Judeans* and at some point shortened to *Jews*). The name was later attached to all the people of Israel as well as their descendents.

The earthly parents of the Christ were also descendants of Abraham and David (People of The Covenant). Old Testament prophecies were made of one who would come through this lineage as a Messiah, a Chosen One, a Savior, to lead the People of The Covenant. Jesus claimed to be this Christ (Messiah). His message originally went to the Jewish descendents of Abraham and David.

Through Christ's sacrificial death and resurrection, the offering of the covenant then went to all those who would accept the Messiah as the Son of God, whether they were Jewish or not (referred to as Gentile). Those who accepted the Son of God were then grafted in, or adopted as sons of God just as the Jewish people were originally sons of God, making all these believers, all these followers of The Way of The Christ, People of The Covenant.

Islam: To the people of Islam, the God of Creation is called *Allah* (The God). Although most Muslims feel it is inappropriate to refer to the religion of Islam as Muhammadanism, they do readily recognize Muhammad as "the prophet through whom Islam reached its definite form," (Smith, 1991, p. 223). And while the religion of Islam believes that Jesus was a prophet of God and even that He was of a virgin birth by the Spirit of God, they believe Muhammad to be a prophet after the Christ—Muhammad being the last prophet.

Islam accepts much of the Biblical Old Testament text, but also believes that the Koran is the later words of God given directly to Muhammad, and therefore supersedes the Bible. Islam does not accept the concept of a Trinity (Father, Son, and Holy Spirit—all of which make up one God).

Muhammad was born A.D. 570. His name means "highly praised." In his forty's, Muhammad felt he received a call from heaven as an appointed prophet of God. Over a period of twenty-three years voices would come to him, take control of his personality, place him in a trance-like state, and in this condition he would speak while those around him recorded what he had to say. These words are what became the Koran and are believed by Muslims to be the final, infallible revelations of God.

Islamic teachings are probably the most specific of the major religions as to their list of what can and cannot be done—even more so than the Bible. Within these teachings are the "Five Pillars of Islam." The first is a confession of faith in no other gods, but Allah. Second is a set prayer schedule—five times per day—as a way to continually remain connected with God. Third is charity—those who have must give generously to those who do not. Forth is an observance of Islam's Holy Month—the month Muhammad initially received his revelation. This ritual includes fasting. The fifth pillar is a pilgrimage, once during a person's life, to Mecca.

One teaching which has received much attention recently is that the Koran does not uphold the Biblical New Testament principal of "turning the other cheek," but rather supports the punishment of wrong and the concept of an approved holy or righteous war. On the other side of the matter, it has likewise been argued that Judaism and even periods of Christianity have a history of warring, or crusading, especially in the defense of spiritual or physical freedom, or to correct worldly wrongs. From his early writings, it appears Muhammad supported religious tolerance, and physical defense—war—was to be utilized only against those who first attacked. However, since his time, the meaning of the Koran's words on a "righteous war" has become clouded and is interpreted in a variety of ways by both Muslims and non-Muslims.

Judaism: To the Hebrew, the Jew, God is Yahweh, often misinterpreted as Jehovah. He is The One Supreme God and Creator of the universe—an always active and personal God. To the Jew, the world was created by this God and is therefore good. Man is the one who continually messes things up and has to be brought back to his Maker.

God's word, to the Jew, is contained in the Old Testament of the Holy Bible, with great emphasis placed on the Torah—the first five books of the Bible. These books, believed to be written by Moses, are Genesis, Exodus, Leviticus, Numbers, and Deuteronomy. Great significance is also placed on the Ten Commandments, found within the book of Exodus.

Traditional Judaism is full of rituals, festivals, and blessings placed on family members and anything else of importance, with much emphasis surrounding the spiritual aspect and sanctity of life. It is a system, however, free of the approved use of "graven images." All worship is to be directed toward the Creator. Within Jewish culture the home and the family become a "sacred place."

Following the directive within the Ten Commandments to keep the Sabbath day, Saturday is to be a day of rest and worship to God. It begins at dark on Friday night and goes through Saturday evening.

The Jewish tradition supports as authentic truth the creation story, as found in Genesis; the story of Noah and the great flood to cleanse the world of sin; the calling of Abraham to become the father of all Jews; the enslaving and breaking free of the ancient Jew from the rule of Egypt; a forty year journey in the wilderness; and a coming into the land of promise, all directed by the hand of God. Traditional Judaism does not, however, believe that the Christ of the New Testament was/is the prophesied Messiah to come and unite the Jewish nation with God.

In and out of a personal relationship with God, up and down in their personal relationship with their countrymen, and in and out of political power, the climax of Judaism is still believed to be in the future coming of The Messiah—the Anointed One, the Chosen One of God—who will provide the Jews with an ultimate triumph over their enemies. There does, however, remain controversy as to whether or not this messiah will be an actual earthy, priestly king or whether God will directly come. And there also exists Jewish Christians, who accept Christ as The Messiah.

While the term Jews actually refers to a Hebrew race of people, Judaism is a religious belief system, to which non-Jews may join themselves.

Christianity: All of Christianity may be summed up in the following three Biblical quotes:

"For God so loved the world that He gave His only begotten Son [Christ], that whoever believes in Him shall not perish, but have eternal life" (NASB, 1995, John 3:16). Jesus, the Christ, is the only leader within the major religions who is claimed to not only have died for His cause, but to have risen from the dead and returned to His Godhead in Heaven.

"No one can come to Me [Christ] unless the Father who sent Me draws him; and I will raise him up on the last day" (NASB, 1995, John 6:44). The only way to God, the Father, is said to be through Christ.

"Do not work for the food which perishes, but for the food which endures to eternal life, which the Son of Man [Christ] will give to you, for on Him the father, God, has set His seal" (NASB, 1995, John 6:27). It is claimed that Christ is the Messiah, the Chosen One of God.

Over the years Christianity has been so perverted by man that in many cases it no longer represents its beginning and its true purpose. Therefore, I will attempt to share with you the traditional meaning and purpose of Christianity as it is outlined in the ancient writings of the Bible.

For all practical purposes Christianity began with the creation, for we are told that the God of creation was actually Three in One—remember that Islam and Judaism also trace their roots back to the creation and the Creator, but for different reasons.

God, or the Godhead, was from the beginning represented by three distinct aspects, sometimes called the Trinity. In Genesis 1, we are told that "In the Beginning *God* created the heavens and the earth" and "the *Spirit of God* moved over the emptiness" before the creation. This God said "let *Us* make man in *Our* image," referring to more than one Godly component or entity (NASB, 1999) [italics added].

John 1:1–13 explains about the 3rd part of God, the Godhead, at the creation: "In the beginning was the *Word*, and the Word was with God, and the Word was God" (NASB, 1999) [italics added]. This Word was also called the *Light*, and the *Christ*—this Word/Light came as a man [flesh—a physical body and mind]. The Word/Light, the Christ, was sent from God to enlighten the world. He was in the world, and the world was made through Him. Those who receive Him become children of God (NASB, 1999).

In Genesis 1:26, we are told that this God (called at times Father, Son, and/or Spirit—all three are noted as God) took dust from the earth (representing the womb of a mother—mother earth), formed a physical man (body and mind), breathed the breath of life (spirit) into this man, and man became a living soul. Man is therefore composed of spirit, soul, mind, and body.

God is manifested in His three forms to help mankind understand His nature(s):

1. **God as a Father.** Think of this as the Soul, or whole, of God. The giver of life. The protector. One from whom we gain an inheritance. One who teaches and guides our lives.

2. **God as a Son**, also called the Word, the Light, and the Christ, represents God coming in physical form. He came in physical form as a human mind and body.

   a. **Son**—representing the union of two—the Son is both man and God—he comes from God and woman. Why? So that He can feel our pain, sorrows, and trials, and understand the difficulty of living in human form. So He can reunite us with our Creator.

   b. **Word**—means the embodying of a concept—a personal manifestation. Christ embodied the attributes of His

Father, in human form and now in written form—the Bible.

c. **Light**—to enlighten/to see clearly/to point the way. Christ came as the Way to the Father.

d. **Christ**—the Anointed One/the Chosen One/Messiah. Christ was the One called by God to lead man homeward.

3. **God as a Spirit**—all that is alive has spirit. God's *Spirit* is sometimes called the Holy Spirit to identify it as different from the creation. The words Spirit of God and Spirit of Christ are used as one (used interchangeably). God and Christ seem to share the same Spirit. Their Spirit is One Spirit. God's Spirit is the ultimate Spirit Guide.

A spirit is the thinking, feeling, and responding aspect of something living. The Spirit of God is the "mind of God"—the thinking, feeling, responding aspect of God.

The words breath, wind, and spirit are used interchangeably—referring to the movement aspect of a spirit. You cannot see it, yet it is there, and it seems to be able to be at more than one place at a time—"absent in body, but present in spirit" (NASB, 1999—I Corinthians 5:3).

The word Christian means Christ-like or follower of Christ. It was first used after Christ's death, around A.D. 63 in Antioch (Acts 11:26). Here it referred to baptized (those immersed in water) believers in the Chosen One, the Anointed One, the Christ. Acts 2:38 says that baptized believers of Christ will be forgiven of their sins, gain eternal life, and receive the indwelling of the Spirit of God/Christ. This Spirit guide is called a helper, a comforter, a guide, a teacher, an advocate, an intercessor, and a seal/guarantee of salvation and eternal life (John 14:16, 26 & Ephesians 1:13).

The spirit of man/woman is believed to know its Creator—it is the spirit that is first touched, aroused. The physical mind sometimes fights the spirit, but if the spirit keeps it up, the spirit will win and convince the mind to listen and follow its lead. In the traditional Christian belief system it is at this point that the individual gives his/her body to be ritually buried (baptism in water) and to rise a new man/women. The Spirit of God then comes to live within the individual, surrounding his/her soul so it will no longer be condemned by the flesh—thus quickening the Spirit, Soul, Mind, and Body of the individual.

The plan of God (Three-In-One), from the creation, was for *all people* to be a chosen race. Many, however, began to move away from their Creator. God's chosen people then became *His followers*—the Jewish race. But these people (as a people) also moved away from God. So God opened a way for *all people* to come back to the Creator, to be enlightened. God would come in a fleshly form, Christ, to bring humankind back to a belief in the Creator. This methodology for spiritual renewal was/is Christianity.

The teachings of Judaism (Old Testament) are called a school master for Christianity—their teachings point to a Chosen One coming to lead the people back. These teachings include directives with the ultimate purpose of showing that humankind cannot make it alone—we need the help and guidance of our Creator.

The Way of Christ has been perverted to include a large list of dos and don'ts by institutions, but it was not, and is not, to be that way. It is to be a *Way of Life*, not a list of what you can and cannot do. It was actually meant to *free us* from rules and guide us to one overwhelming directive which will forever enlighten us.

"And you are to love the Lord your God [Creator—Father, Son, Spirit] with all your heart [spirit], and with all your soul, and with all your mind, and with all your strength [body]." And a second directive: "You shall love your neighbor as yourself. There is no other command greater than these" (NASB, 1999—Mark 12:30-31). How shall we accomplish these decrees? "By the power of the Holy Spirit" (NASB, 1999 — Romans 8:13 & 15:13). God's Spirit, which now lives within us, gives us the ability to love and to accomplish whatever God puts before us. We do not have to do it of our own ability, for we now have the power of our Creator guiding us, directing us, and bringing about goodness through us.

In simple terms, Christianity is: believing in the Soul of God (the Father) and gaining access to the Soul of God through a belief in His physical manifestation (the Son of God — Jesus). Both will then unite and live within us in Spirit form (the Holy Spirit). This Spirit will then guide us and direct us, becoming our personal Spirit Guide, in finding our purpose, in loving and serving others, and in making the world a better place to live. By allowing God to work in and through us, we become Christians — we become: **The Way of The Christ.**

❖ ❖ ❖

"The individual who is not anchored in God can offer no resistance on his own resources to the physical and moral blandishments of the world. For this he needs the evidence of inner, transcendent experience which alone can protect him from the otherwise inevitable submersion in the mass" (Jung, 1957, p. 34).

❖ ❖ ❖

BIBLIOGRAPHY

Adair, J. (1775). *History of the American Indians.* Reprinted in: Samual Cole Williams, (Ed). Johnson City, TN: Wautauga Press, 1930.

Aquinas, T. (1968). *The pocket Aquinas.* Edited by Vernon J. Bourke. New York: Washington Square Press.

Bear Heart. (1998). *The wind is my mother — the life and teachings of a Native American shaman.* New York: Berkley Books.

Campbell, J. (1988). *The power of myth — with Bill Moyers.* New York: Doubleday.

Chambers, O. (1995). *My utmost for His highest.* Edited by James Reimann. Grand Rapids, MI: Discovery House Publishers.

Chief Seattle. (1855). A message from Chief Seattle. Reprinted in: Susan Jeffers, *Brother Eagle, Sister Sky.* New York: Scholastic Inc., 1992.

Dalai Lama. (2002). *How to practice the way to a meaningful life.* Translated and Edited by Jeffery Hopkins, Ph.D., New York: Pocket Books.

Dalai Lama. (2003). *365 daily advice from the heart.* Translated by Dominque Messent, Edited by Matthieu Rocard. London: Element — Harper Collins Publishers.

de Chardin, T. (1975). *The phenomenon of man.* New York: Harper and Row.

Fire/Lame Deer & Erodoes R. (1972). *Lame Deer seeker of visions.* New York: Pocket Books.

Flew, A. (1979). *A dictionary of Philosophy*. New York: St. Martin's Press.

Gaarder, J. (1996). *Sophie's world*. London: Phoenix, a division of Orian Books Ltd.

Garrett J.T. (2001). *The Cherokee: Prayers, songs, and stories of healing and harmony*. Rochester, Vermont: Bear & Company Publishing

Garrett J.T. & Garrett M. (1996). *Medicine of the Cherokee: The way of right relationship*. Rochester, Vermont: Bear & Company Publishing.

Garrett J.T. & Garrett M. (2002). *The Cherokee full circle: A practical guide to ceremonies and traditions*. Rochester, Vermont: Bear & Company Publishing.

Garrett M. (1998). *Walking on the wind: Cherokee teachings for harmony and balance*. Rochester, Vermont: Bear & Company Publishing.

Healing Touch Level I Training Notebook. (1996). Carrboro, NC: North Carolina Center for Healing Touch.

Hill, R.B. (1979). *Hanta Yo*. New York: Warner Books.

Hilliard, K.M. (2002). *The catcher of dreams: A holistic approach to wellness therapy*. Franklin, Tennessee: O'More Publishing.

Holy Bible, Easy to Read Version. (2000). Fort Worth, Texas: World Bible Translation Center.

Jung, C.G. (1959). *The undiscovered self*. New York: New American Library.

Kilpatrick, A.E. (1991). Going to water: A structural analysis of Cherokee purifications rituals. *American Indian Culture and Research Journal*, 15(2), 49-58.

Kolak, D. (1997). *Lovers of wisdom: A historical introduction to philosophy*. Belmont, CA: Wadsworth Publishing Company.

Kulananda. (2001). *Buddhism*. London: Thorsons – HarperCollins Publishers.

Lehew, C. (2003). *Metaphysics 101: Manifesting your dreams*. Franklin, Tennessee: Greysmith Publishing, Inc.

Life. (1957). *The world's great religions.* New York: Time Incorporated.

Mails, T.E. (1988). *Secret Native American pathways: A guide to inner peace.* Tulsa, Oklahoma: Council Oak Books.

Mails, T.E. (1991). *Fools Crow: Wisdom and power.* Tulsa Oklahoma: Council Oak Books.

Mails, T.E. (1996). *The Cherokee People.* New York: Malowe & Co.

Marden, O.S. (1913). *The joys of living.* New York: Thomas Y. Crowell Company.

McLuhan, T.C. (1971). *Touch the earth: A self-portrait of Indian existence.* New York: Simon and Schuster.

Mooney, J. (1891). *Sacred formulas of the Cherokee.* Seventh annual report of the Bureau of American Ethnology of the Smithsonian Institution. Washington, DC: Government Printing Office.

Mooney, J. (1891). *Sacred formulas of the Cherokee.* Reprinted in: G. Ellison, (Ed), History, myths, and sacred formulas of the Cherokee. Ashville, NC: Bright Mountain Books, 1992.

Mooney, J. (1891). *Myths of the Cherokee.* Reprinted in: G. Ellison, (Ed), History, myths, and sacred formulas of the Cherokee. Ashville, NC: Bright Mountain Books, 1992.

Neihardt, J. (1995). *Black Elk speaks.* Lincoln and London: University of Nebraska Press.

New American Standard Bible. (1999). Grand Rapids, Michigan: Zondervan Publishing House.

Osbon, D.K. (1991). *Reflections on the art of living: A Joseph Campbell companion.* New York: HarperCollins Publishers Inc.

Payne, J.H. (N.d.) *Payne manuscripts.* Vol. 1-14. Chicago, IL: Newberry Library.

Peck, M.S. (1978). *The road less traveled: A new psychology of love, traditional values and spiritual growth.* New York: Simon and Schuster.

Peck, M.S. (1993). *The road less traveled: The unending journey toward spiritual growth.* New York: Simon and Schuster.

Plato. (1942). *Five great dialogues.* Translated by B. Jowett, Edited by Louise Ropes Loomis. New York: The Classics Club, Walter J. Black.

Sanford, A. (1982). *The healing gifts of the Spirit.* New York: Jove.

Sanford, A. (1983). *The healing power of the Bible.* New York: Jove.

Sanford, A. (1991). *The healing light.* New York: Ballatine.

Self Healing Newsletter. (January, 2005). *Fasting: A fresh start toward better health.* Marion, OH: Body & Soul Omnimedia, Inc.

Smith, H. (1991). *The world's religions.* New York: HarperCollins Publishers Inc.

Stolzman, W. (1998). *The pipe and Christ.* Chamberlain, South Dakota: Tipi Press.

Stumpf, S.E. (1993). *Elements of philosophy.* New York: McGraw-Hill, Inc.

Thoreau, H. (1965). *Walden: Essay on civil disobedience.* New ork: Airmont Publishing Co.

Thoreau, H. (2000). *Thoreau: A book of quotations.* Edited by:General Editor Paul Negri, Editor of this volume Bob Blaisdell. New York: Dover Publishing, Inc.

Walsh, R. (1999). *Essential spirituality: The 7 central practices to awaken heart and mind.* New York: John Wiley & Sons, Inc.

Warner, R. (1958). *The Greek philosophers.* New York: Mentor.

Warren, R. (2002). *The purpose driven life.* Grand Rapids, MI: Zondervan.

ABOUT THE AUTHOR

Hilliard's doctoral training includes an emphasis in higher education that deeply embraces the *art and philosophy* of teaching and learning, but he specialized in wellness—a field of *science* which includes psychology, physiology, sociology, and the metaphysical field of spirituality. As such, he trained in both the arts and the sciences and believes these two disciplines complement each other and that they necessitate unity in order for higher learning to occur. Hilliard believes, "When appropriately joined together, the art and science of teaching and learning create *educational wellness*." Professor Hilliard's training also includes years of research into Native American cultures and learning styles (specifically the Eastern Band of the Cherokee and the Lakota) that highly incorporate individualized sensory, intuitive, and spiritual philosophies of teaching and learning.

Because of his scholarly research, in the summer of 2006, Dr. Hilliard was invited by the Oxford Round Table, Jesus College, University of Oxford, England, to present his research on Educational Wellness (specifically his *Hilliard Circle of Teaching and Learning Theory*) before a group of forty educators from around the world. He returned to the

University of Oxford, Harris Manchester College, as a Visiting Research Scholar and Fellow in June 2007, 2010, 2013, and 2014 to further his studies on sensory teaching and learning.

Dr. Hilliard served as President and CEO of O'More College of Design in Franklin, Tennessee, and was a distinguished professor of Educational Wellness, Marriage and Family, Holistic Wellness, and Spirituality. He is currently the Vice Chancellor, President, and Professor of The Hilliard Institute; Visiting Fellow, Harris Manchester College, University of Oxford; and Director-General, The Oxford Centre for the Study of Law and Public Policy.

www.ingramcontent.com/pod-product-compliance
Lightning Source LLC
Chambersburg PA
CBHW030046100426
42734CB00036B/251